God's Final WARNING to America

John McTernan can be contacted by writing:
P.O. Box 444
Liverpool, PA 17045

or by e-mail:
cops4c@aol.com

Printed in the United States of America

ISBN 1-57558-27-6

God's Final
WARNING
to America

John McTernan

Table of Contents

Foreword To Third Printing

On October 11, 1987, I was watching the evening news. The broadcast covered a huge homosexual gathering in Washington, D.C. There were up to 500,000 homosexuals and supporters at this rally. It may have been up to that time the largest gathering of homosexuals in history. I turned off the television and walked away. I never thought that such an event might offend my holy God. The thought of prayer and intercession before God about this rally never entered my mind. I quickly forgot this event.

The week following this rally witnessed the greatest one-week stock market decline in the market's history. Then on October 19, exactly six working days after this rally, the market crashed 508 points. That night I watched the evening news. The news reporter was visibly upset and asked if this crash would be the start of an economic depression. As I watched the news reporter, my mind flashed back to the homosexual rally only a few days before. I then sensed this strong voice in my mind. The powerful impression was that the stock market collapse was timed with the homosexual rally, and the crash was judgment on America. The impression was overwhelmingly strong that more judgment was coming to America. If America continued on this course of boldly proclaiming sin, awesome judgment was coming to the point where the country would be destroyed.

At that moment, I realized I did not understand the

holiness of God. I lacked a real fear of God concerning sin. When I realized this, I immediately repented. I fell on the floor and confessed my callousness toward God's holiness and that I lacked a true fear of Him. From that day forward, I began to see the correlation between national events against God's Word and disasters. These disasters usually hit the very day of the event, or within a day or two. This book documents this correlation between America's rebellion against God and the subsequent disasters hitting the country.

In August 1992, I watched Hurricane Andrew smash into Florida. This hurricane was the greatest natural disaster to hit America. This hurricane hit the very day the Madrid peace process moved to America and met for the first time. From that day forward, I began to see awesome disasters hit America to the very day the president was pressuring Israel to give away God's covenant land.

The object of this book is to draw attention that God is warning America in a very real way. God always warns a nation before He moves in judgment. As you read this book, you will see that America has been warned. This book shows the authority and reality of God's Word. The Bible is to be taken seriously.

The church in America has lost the understanding of how holy God is, and that a nation can offend the holiness of God. When the holiness of God is lost, the true fear of God is lost with it. God is holy and when it comes to sin, to be feared.

My hope is this book will be used by the church to realize the holiness of God and turn to Him in true repentance. The warnings of God detailed in the book would cause fervent prayer and intercession. It will result in the courage of Christians to stand for life, the family and God's covenant people Israel.

—John McTernan, August 2000

Chapter One

The Warning Judgments

Since the mid-1980s, America has suffered one awesome disaster after another. There have always been disasters, but now they are happening regularly and with greater intensity. The media is constantly reporting such dramatic headlines as: "The Worst Flooding in 500 Years," "The Worst Stock Market Crash in History," "The Worst Tornadoes This Century," "The Most Destructive Hurricane on Record," "The Most Powerful Earthquake in 80 Years," "The Worst Year Ever for Forest Fires," "The Coldest Winter on Record," and "The Worst Ice Storm This Century." The list of these headlines dramatizing the disasters hitting America can go on and on. These headlines cover only a 10-year period of time! Think of what has happened to America since 1987.

In October 1987, the stock market plummeted over 500 points, which to that time was the greatest crash in history. The effect of this crash was felt well into the 1990s. The Midwest and especially California, suffered the worst drought in history, destroying huge amounts of crops. The drought was then followed by record rains and severe flooding in both sections. In 1989, Hurricane Hugo struck Charleston, South Carolina, with fierce winds causing great damage. Soon after Hugo hit, a powerful earthquake rocked San Francisco causing great damage.

In the year 1992, incredible events occurred. Four powerful earthquakes hit California. These quakes were all in remote areas, so the damage was not severe. In fact, 10 of the most powerful quakes in the world during 1992 were centered in California—including the most powerful earthquake that year at 7.6 magnitude. This quake was centered near the major faults of southern California. Hurricane Andrew was one of the most powerful and destructive hurricanes ever to hit the country. This hurricane was the most expensive natural disaster in American history. The worst rioting since the Civil War took place in Los Angeles. A record number of tornadoes swept across America. Record forest fires raged throughout the West, especially in California.

The year 1993 saw record northeastern storms tear at the East Coast causing severe damage and flooding. One of the worst terrorist attacks in American history struck New York City. This was soon followed by the worst day in federal law enforcement history as four agents were killed and 16 were wounded near Waco, Texas. The worst flooding ever ravaged the Midwest. Scientists described the flood as the type which occurs once every 500 years. California was again hit with record wildfires.

The incredible disasters continued into 1994. The coldest temperatures ever recorded covered the Midwest and East. The records were started in the 1880s. Record cold temperatures were set in hundreds of locations. The cold was so intense that the wind chill hit near 90 degrees below zero in some locations. Cold and snow paralyzed entire states. Pennsylvania was hit by the most powerful earthquake in the state's history. The quake was mild by California standards, registering only 4.6, but Pennsylvania is not an earthquake prone area. The epicenter of the quake was Reading, and it was felt as far away as Philadelphia and New York City. Two days later, a powerful earthquake measuring 6.8 magnitude struck Los Angeles, causing tremendous damage. This earthquake was the second most costly natural disaster, close behind the awesome destruction of Hurricane Andrew. The East Coast was first rocked by an earthquake, followed by the West Coast two days later.

In March 1994, devastating tornadoes, some of the worst this century, first struck Alabama and then spread throughout the South. In June, the value of the American dollar plummeted to an all-time low against many foreign currencies, causing the stock market to fall. (In one week, the stock market lost $200 billion.) In July, Tropical Storm Alberto dumped 21 inches of rain in one day on the state of Georgia, causing the worst flooding in over 100 years. In addition, all summer huge forest fires burned throughout many of the western states. Over three million acres of forests were burned by the fires. In October, a tropical storm stalled over southeastern Texas. The storm dumped almost 30 inches of rain in three days on the Houston area, paralyzing huge sections of Texas. In November, Tropical Storm Gordon hit Florida and did tremendous damage to the winter vegetable crop. Also in November, a political earthquake hit America, as the election broke the 40-year hold the Democratic Party had on Congress. The change was so dramatic that even the Speaker of the House of Representatives was defeated in the general election. This was the first time the Speaker was not reelected as a congressman since 1861. In December, Orange County, California, went bankrupt as it lost over $1.5 billion in the bond market. This was the greatest failure of a county government in United States history.

In January 1995, powerful storms pummeled California. A series of powerful storms hit the entire state causing upward of $1.3 billion in damage. Torrential rains caused severe flooding throughout the entire state. The storms even caused tornadoes. Tornadoes are extremely rare in California, but occurring in January is very odd. Scientists stated the torrential rains and flooding that hit California were so powerful, they occur only once every 500 years. These were awesome storms. The worst terrorist attack in United States history destroyed the Federal Building in Oklahoma City. In August, Hurricane Erin hit the Florida panhandle. In October, powerful Hurricane Opal also slammed into nearly the same location on the Florida panhandle.

The winter of 1996 proved to be the most severe on record since records were kept. This winter was worse than 1994. The spring brought severe flooding to the West because of the snow melt. In May the newspapers were reporting that the worst drought since the 1930s was gripping the Great Plains. In July, Hurricane Bertha slammed into North Carolina, and in September powerful Hurricane Fran, amazingly, hit the same location in North Carolina.

In 1997, the West was again hit with record snow and rain, causing severe flooding and mud slides. Awesome tornadoes destroyed the small towns of Arkadelphia, Arkansas and Jarred, Texas. These towns were literally destroyed. In March, powerful storms caused record flooding along the Ohio River. The town of Falmouth, Kentucky, was destroyed. In April, the spring thaw caused record flooding along the Red River in the Dakotas. Grand Rapids, North Dakota, was totally destroyed by the flood. The Ohio and Red River floods were described by scientists as 500-year floods. In July, Hurricane Danny formed overnight in the Gulf of Mexico. It hit Alabama, dumping 30 inches of rain. On October 27, the stock market crashed 554 points for the greatest one-day point crash in history.

The National Climatic Data Center (NCDC) has documented the billion-dollar weather related disasters that have hit America between 1980 and May 1997. These disasters included hurricanes, floods, droughts, blizzards, and freezes. The NCDC identified 30 disasters during this period. Of the 30 disasters, 25 occurred between 1988 and

1997, while 21 occurred during the August 1992 to May 1997 period. There has been a great intensifying of the disasters.

Between 1980 and 1991, the nation averaged one billion-dollar disaster a year. This included all forms of disasters. From 1992 to 1997, the average was four disasters (billion dollars or greater) a year, with five occurring in 1995. The increase in billion-dollar disasters has been fourfold since 1992!

These disasters have cost hundreds of billions of dollars and have weakened many institutions, like the insurance industry. Tens of thousands of people have been left homeless, and thousands of businesses have been destroyed. In some cases, entire states were affected by these disasters.

In the mid-1980s, America went from being a creditor nation to the 1990s when it became the world's **greatest debtor nation**. By 1993, the U.S. Commerce Department reported America owed foreign investors $555.7 billion. The years 1991 and 1992 saw the most severe recession since the Great Depression of the 1930s; and California, for the first time since the Great Depression, went bankrupt. Many other states were in their worst financial condition since the Great Depression. Mass murders and serial killings, which were rare in America 30 years ago, now seem to be a regular occurrence in the 1990s.

These events are not happening by coincidence; they are warnings from God. Americans are now either practicing or tolerating lifestyles which the Bible clearly states will remove God's blessings and bring the wrath of God. God has warned in the Bible that He will destroy any nation which openly practices fornication, adultery, homosexuality, sexual perversion, and the shedding of the blood of innocent children. The shedding of the blood of children includes abortion. Concerning abortion, the Bible makes no distinction between a child in the womb and a newly born baby.

The following Bible verses show God's attitude toward a nation that practices open sin:

> Moreover thou shall not lie carnally with your neighbor's wife, to defile thyself with her. And thou shalt not let any of thy seed pass through the fire to Molech [this is child sacrifice]. . . . Thou shalt not lie with mankind, as with womankind: it is abomination. Neither shalt thou lie with any beast to defile thyself therewith: . . . Defile not ye yourselves in any of these things: for in all these the nations are defiled which I cast out before you: And the land is defiled: therefore I do visit the iniquity thereof upon it, and the land itself vomiteth out her inhabitants.
>
> —Leviticus 18:20–25

> He turneth rivers into a wilderness and the watersprings into dry ground, a fruitful land into barrenness **for the wickedness of them that dwell therein.**
>
> —Psalms 107:33–34

Since the mid-1980s, America has been severely warned by God that, as a nation, we are on a collision course with Him. God is extremely merciful and long-suffering. He will warn and warn before judgment; but if a nation will not turn from open homosexuality and the shedding of the blood of innocent children, His holiness demands judgment on that nation. The Bible records the total destruction of the cities of Sodom and Gomorrah as an example of what happens to a nation that practices open sexual immorality, but especially homosexuality:

> Even as Sodom and Gomorrah, and the cities about them in like manner, giving themselves over to fornication, and

going after strange flesh, are set forth for an example, suffering the vengeance of eternal fire.

—Jude 7

A careful study of the events surrounding many of these disasters, especially the stock market crashes, major earthquakes, and hurricanes, reveal they all occurred in connection with abortion and/or homosexual-related events. God has sent clear warnings. These disasters serve as warnings because the nation has recovered. The disasters have not yet permanently damaged America. The disasters which have occurred are for national repentance. They are warnings to lead Americans to repentance. In this sense, the disasters can be viewed as "warning-judgments." God in His mercy has sent many clear warnings.

The following examples document that America has already been clearly warned by God for shedding the blood of innocent children in the womb and sexual immorality including open homosexuality. These warnings show America is on a collision course with our holy God and awesome judgment lies just ahead. No more warnings from God may be forthcoming. The next round of judgments could devastate the nation.

The examples of the warning-judgments which have fallen on America since October 1987 follow:

The Warning-Judgments

October 1987

On October 19, 1987, the stock market dropped over 500 points for the greatest one-day crash in history. The crash resulted in a one-day drop of 22.6 percent in the market and a loss of over $500 billion. By comparison, the crash on October 28, 1929, which was attributed as the start of the Great Depression, was only 12.6 percent. The effect of the 1987 crash was felt well into the 1990s. The U.S.

economy was increasing at a six percent rate during October 1987, but as a direct result of the crash it contracted to a negative four percent by 1990.

Just eight days before the stock market crash on October 11, 1987, probably the largest gathering of homosexuals in world history took place in Washington, D.C. The newspapers reported that over 200,000 people marched past the White House and gathered near the Capitol. Some reports claimed the marchers numbered 500,000. The homosexuals were marching to end discrimination and increase funding for AIDS research. The newspapers reported the crowd carried signs stating, "Thank God I'm Gay," and "Condoms, Not Condemnation." Others were saying, "I'm gay and I'm proud." Has there ever been a time in history when such a huge group of homosexuals gathered in a nation's capital to demand their rights?

God answered this march, just eight days later, with the greatest stock market crash in U.S. history. In fact, the week immediately following the homosexual march, the stock market dropped 235 points. For the eight days immediately following the march, the stock market dropped 735 points for a loss of 32.1 percent! October 1987 marked the high-water mark for the U.S. economy as it was growing at over six percent. After the crash, the economy began to contract until it hit a low of negative four percent growth in the fall of 1990. The economy contracted 10 percent in just three years! With the size of the economy, this resulted in the loss of hundreds of billions of dollars. As late as August 1992, the newspapers reported 20 percent of the stocks had not recovered from the crash. The recession of 1991 and 1992 can be traced primarily to the crash of 1987. Many American firms downsized after the crash and hundreds of thousands of jobs were lost. This crash had a powerful impact on the economy. The downsizing of corporations continued into the late 1990s. The crash permanently changed the face of corporate America.

God shook America with a powerful economic warning. On October 19, 1987, America had an economic "heart attack!" This "heart attack" happened just eight days after the massive homosexual rally! The crash of 1987 did not result in a 1930s-type depression. America survived the crash, but continued to amass huge amounts of debt. America went into huge amounts of debt to keep the economy from a depression. By the late 1990s, the federal government was over $5.1 trillion in debt. The combined debt of all levels of government—plus corporations and individuals—totals over $11 trillion and is growing fast. This debt could prove to be a burden from which the nation can not escape.

The homosexuals marched in the nation's capital, and the entire country was shaken through the stock market crash. The largest gathering of homosexuals in history was immediately followed by one of the greatest stock market crashes in history. This timing of these events was no coin-

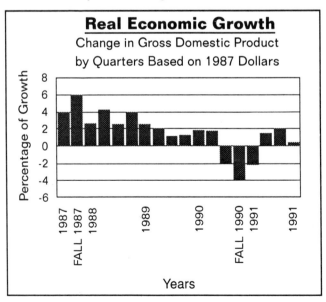

Real Economic Growth
Change in Gross Domestic Product
by Quarters Based on 1987 Dollars

cidence! America continues in many ways to promote and encourage the homosexual lifestyle. The surest and quickest way to touch the entire nation is through the economy and especially the stock market. God has clearly warned America about the promotion of open homosexuality. The next stock market crash of this magnitude could devastate the economy and completely alter America forever.

September 1989

On Friday, September 22, 1989, Hurricane Hugo slammed into Charleston, South Carolina, causing tremendous damage to the city and the entire state. The winds were recorded around 135 mph, and the headlines in the newspapers referred to Hugo as a "monster storm." Hurricane Hugo was classified as a Category 4 in power. The damage from Hugo would total over $7 billion.

On Thursday, September 21, 1989, the *Washington Post* had a front-page article about Hugo approaching the United States. The article was titled "Troops Ordered to Calm Virgin Islands," subtitled "Looting Continues: Hurricane Expected to hit Mainland **Friday**." The next day the storm's eye struck right near Charleston.

The *Washington Post* also on September 21 had a front-page article about abortion. This article was actually touching and directly underneath the Hurricane Hugo article. The article was titled "U.S. May Forego Request for Abortion Review," subtitled "Administration Faces **Friday** Deadline for Action in Minnesota Case." The article went on to explain the Bush Administration only had until **Friday** (the next day) to make oral arguments before the Supreme Court in the *Hodgson v. Minnesota* case. The oral argument was for the possibility of overturning *Roe v. Wade*, and thus end legalized abortion in America. The oral argument was never made, and *Roe v. Wade* was not overturned.

It is ironic that a national newspaper should have two

front-page articles—one dealing with abortion and the second with Hurricane Hugo—literally touching each other. Very few hurricanes with the power of Hugo have hit America. There are very few cases that are argued before the Supreme Court which could overturn legalized abortion. What are the odds of a hurricane like Hugo hitting the United States the very same day the government foregoes the opportunity to overturn *Roe v. Wade?*

October 1989

On October 12, 1989, the nation's newspapers had headlines that the United States House of Representatives had provided funds to pay for a poor woman to obtain an abortion. On this same day, the Florida legislature refused to pass any laws restricting abortions. The Florida legislature's failure to pass laws restricting abortion was very significant. Earlier in the year, on July 3, 1989, the Supreme Court in *Webster v. Reproductive Health Service* ruled that states could restrict abortion.

Florida was the first state to attempt to make substantial restrictions of abortion, and the governor had promised he would sign into law any restrictions the legislature passed. The Florida legislature was being watched by the entire nation, and what happened in Florida had national implications. The failure of the legislature to pass any restrictions was a significant pro-abortion victory. Immediately following these pro-abortion victories, on October 13, 1989, the stock market again crashed. The market fell 190 points in one day, for a loss of seven percent. Actually, the crash occurred in just one hour at the end of the day. At that time, it was the twelfth greatest crash in history.

Two days later, on October 15, 1989, the governors of 10 states urged the Supreme Court to strike down an Illinois state law restricting abortion. The governors signed a friend-of-the-court brief, claiming the law would impose

"extremely burdensome requirements on abortion clinics."
The governors were from Colorado, Vermont, Maine, Michigan, Ohio, Alaska, New York, Massachusetts, Washington, and Oregon.

Also on October 15, 1989, a huge pro-abortion rally took place in San Francisco. The crowd was estimated at 50,000. The *San Francisco Chronicle* reported the rally in a front-page article titled "Huge Abortion-Rights Rally in SF." The paper reported the rally was festive and came in the aftermath of several recent pro-abortion victories. In describing the rally, the paper stated, "Marching to a pounding drum and chanting, Hear our voice we're pro-choice, yesterday's crowd gathered at City Hall after passing cheering supporters lined up along Market Street." The center of the rally was **City Hall**, where many pro-abortion politicians addressed the crowd. The politicians included Diane Feinstein and Barbara Boxer, both of whom were later elected as senators from California.

Just two days after this festive rally celebrating the killing of innocent children in the womb, a powerful earthquake struck near San Francisco. This quake was 7.1 magnitude, and it was the fifth most powerful this century to hit America. This quake actually struck during a baseball World Series game and was broadcast live to the nation. Literally millions of Americans watched as the earthquake shook San Francisco. Although the earthquake was extremely powerful, miraculously very few people died. Ironically, the *San Francisco Chronicle*, reporting on the effect of the quake, said that **City Hall** was shaken so terribly that people fled the building screaming in terror. The paper reported, "At City Hall in San Francisco a radio reporter told listeners, 'The entire building started to shake . . . you could hear people yelling and screaming all over the building.'" The very center of the festive, pro-abortion rally became, just two days later, a center of terror and fear!

The pro-abortion victories were followed two days later by the stock market crash. The huge pro-abortion rally in San Francisco and the pro-abortion statement by the governors were followed two days later by the fifth most powerful earthquake this century. The stock market crash and then the earthquake hitting the very location of the rally were not coincidences. They were powerful warnings that the killing of children in the womb has America on a collision course with God.

August 1991

During the summer of 1991, the pro-life organization Operation Rescue held a national event at the abortion center of George Tiller in Wichita, Kansas. The event was called the Summer of Mercy. Tiller specializes in late-term abortions. Tiller even has an incinerator on site to burn the bodies of the aborted babies. Women come from all over America and even foreign countries to him for late-term abortions. Tiller's practice is not only local, but covers the entire nation. The height of the event was in August. There were over 2,600 people arrested at Tiller's abortion center for peacefully trying to block the entrance. A rally on August 25 drew 35,000. This was a massive national pro-life event to try and stop the killing of babies.

On August 18, at the height of this event powerful Hurricane Bob brushed North Carolina, and on August 19–20 slammed into New England. This hurricane caused over $1 billion in damage. On August 20, *USA Today* reported that Hurricane Bob had slammed into New England. The destruction of Hurricane Bob was reported in a nearly full-page article titled "Bob batters Eastern Seaboard." At the bottom of this article was a report on this national pro-life event. The article was titled "Abortion foes flock to 'Heartland' rally." The article next to the one about Hurricane Bob was titled "Court challenges military ban on gays." The article about Hurricane Bob was flanked by articles about homosexuality and abortion

April 1992
The month started with one of the largest pro-abortion rallies ever to take place. On April 5, 1992, a crowd estimated at 500,000 marched in Washington for abortion rights. The *Washington Post* reported that the rally was one of the largest political events in the city's history. This rally was also festive, and tens of thousands of the marchers were homosexuals and lesbians. The rally was to protest the upcoming Supreme Court hearing of the *Planned Parenthood v. Casey* case. This hearing was to take place later in the month.

The Casey case was a result of Pennsylvania's passage of the Abortion Control Act of 1989, which Planned Parenthood had challenged. The Abortion Control Act contained provisions that a woman had to wait 24 hours before obtaining an abortion, and she had to be provided with information about the development of her unborn child. There was much speculation in the major news sources that the Supreme Court would use this case to overturn legalized abortion.

On April 20, 1992, Operation Rescue began a 10-day event called Spring of Life in Buffalo, New York, to try and peacefully close the abortion centers so babies would not be killed. Operation Rescue is a nonviolent, Christian organization that uses peaceful means to block the entrances to abortion centers. This is done in an attempt to persuade mothers to keep their child and to prevent unborn babies from being killed. This event received national attention, and pro-abortion supporters came from all over the United States to insure that the babies would be killed. Three days later, on April 23, the United States Supreme Court heard the *Planned Parenthood v. Casey* case.

While Operation Rescue was taking place in Buffalo

and the court was hearing the abortion case, a powerful 6.3 magnitude earthquake shook southern California. This was the fourteenth most powerful earthquake this century to hit California. The epicenter of this earthquake was in a place called Joshua Tree, an isolated desert area, so the damage was minimal; however, it shook most of the southwestern part of the country. The Joshua Tree earthquake actually occurred the same day that the Supreme Court heard the abortion case. This was not a coincidence.

On April 25, 1992, during a fierce counterprotest in Buffalo against Operation Rescue, a 7.1 magnitude earthquake hit California. The Petrolia earthquake was the sixth most powerful this century. The earthquake was in a remote section and again not much damage was done; however, huge sections of the northwest were rocked by the quake's power.

A newspaper reported the fierceness of the pro–abortion supporters and homosexuals in their counter protest. The paper reported: "Only the rows of Erie County sheriffs and Buffalo police prevented violence as abortion supporters roared themselves into a frenzy with bone-chilling chants." One of the chants was, "Kill the Christians." The counter protest was lead by homosexuals and lesbians who sang such vile songs as, "God Is a Lesbian, God Is a Dyke" to the tune of "My Country 'Tis of Thee," and "There Is No Room in My Womb for You and Me" to the tune of "This Land Is Your Land." These people were openly mocking God and viciously degrading unborn children in the womb!

Also during the 10 days of Operation Rescue's Spring of Life, the jury in California was deliberating the verdict of the police officers who beat Rodney King. Operation Rescue ended on April 29, 1992, with fierce opposition from pro-abortionists and homosexuals. This very same day, April 29, 1992, the jury made its decision to acquit the police officers and Los Angeles immediately went up in flames.

Rioting also broke out in several other cities throughout the nation.

The month started with a huge, festive pro-abortion rally in the nation's capital, and ended with Los Angeles, one of America's largest cities, up in flames. Two massive earthquakes, plus the worst rioting since the Civil War, took place during this 10-day event to save the lives of the innocent unborn. These two earthquakes occurred while homosexuals and pro-abortion supporters mocked God and His people who were trying to save babies. This was not a coincidence. These quakes shook the western section of the nation. An earthquake occurring on the day of the Supreme Court hearing was also not a coincidence.

The timing of the earthquakes and the rioting starting exactly as Operation Rescue ended are clear warning–judgments—that the killing of innocent children in the womb and mocking God, has America on a collision course with God.

June 1992

On June 28, 1992, hundreds of thousands of homosexuals and their supporters attended national Gay Pride Day parades across America. The last Sunday in June has been designated as Gay Pride Day. Almost all the major cities hold parades celebrating homosexuality. Hundreds of thousands turn out to march and support the homosexuals.

On the very morning of Gay Pride Day, the fourth and ninth most powerful earthquakes this century hit southern California. These quakes were so powerful, their effects were felt as far away as Idaho. The *Los Angeles Times* actually reported that the marchers had to brave the earthquakes to get to the Gay Pride Day parade.

The fourth most powerful quake was 7.6 magnitude and was called the Landers quake because it occurred near Landers, California. The Landers quake was the most powerful earthquake in the world during 1992. This was an awesome earthquake. The force of this quake ruptured the earth for 53 miles. The second quake, called Big Bear, was 6.5 magnitude. Both of the earthquakes were in remote areas, so California was spared from great loss of life and extensive damage. These quakes were dangerously close to the San Andreas' fault line. If an earthquake occurred on this fault, it could devastate California.

Scientists studying the Landers quake were astonished by its impact on the entire western section of the nation. The March 1993 issue of *Earth Magazine* contained an article titled "Lessons from Landers." This article documented how bizarre and powerful this earthquake really was. Excerpts from this article follow. One geologist said in the article, "I think the Landers event will go down in history as one of the most important earthquakes from a scientific standpoint." The scientists found that the Landers quake was bizarre. They reported,

> Landers was not only powerful—it was bizarre. In most earthquakes, the land tears along a single fault. But not this quake, the rupture hopscotched from fault to fault, growing more powerful with each successive jump.

The scientists reported the strange phenomenon that immediately followed the Landers quake, a swarm of smaller quakes that jolted the entire West. The Landers quake triggered smaller quakes in northern California, Idaho, Utah, Nevada, and even 750 miles away in Yellowstone National Park. Small earthquakes were detected minutes after the Landers quake under Lassen Peak and Mount Shasta, both in northern California. Both of these mountains are volcanoes. A magnitude 5.5 quake struck in southern Nevada. The scientists reported that "in the past most scientists would have scoffed at suggestions that one quake could trigger activity at such great distances."

One scientist stated, "So many areas became active— as if someone had flicked on a switch. Tremors started in regions hundreds of miles away from southern California mere seconds after the Landers quake." This was the first time scientists ever detected that an earthquake set off other quakes hundreds of miles away! The scientists had no explanation for the distant earthquake-triggering phenomenon of the Landers quake! The Landers quake was unique. This is why the Landers quake was said to go down in history as the most important from a scientific standpoint.

What a powerfully clear warning from God! During the very morning of Gay Pride Day, two powerful earthquakes literally shook the entire West Coast of America. Ironically the very next day, the Supreme Court handed down the *Planned Parenthood v. Casey* decision, which failed to overturn the legalization of abortion. It seems one earthquake was for Gay Pride Day and the second was for the Supreme Court decision. How much clearer can the warning–judgments from God be!

A major earthquake hit southern California on April 23, 1992—the day the Supreme Court heard the *Planned Parenthood v. Casey* case. Just two months later, the very day before the decision, the fourth and ninth most powerful earthquakes this century hit southern California. There seems to be a clear spiritual connection between the quakes and the Supreme Court's involvement in this abortion case.

It is extremely noteworthy that scientists who study earthquakes believe the earthquakes on April 23 and June 28, 1992, were connected. The *Los Angeles Times* reported this connection in a January 20, 1994, article titled "Scientists Ponder Northward Concentration of Quakes." In this article scientists were quoted as saying:

> Frequent aftershocks following the magnitude 6.3 Joshua
> Tree quake of April 23, 1992, migrated in a northwestern

direction and appeared to some scientists to have triggered the much larger 7.6 Landers quake of June 28, 1992.

The earthquakes appear connected, and the earthquake on April 23 actually set up the powerful quake on June 28. Can all this be a coincidence?

These earthquakes were both physically and spiritually connected! They were linked together and occurred almost the very same day the Supreme Court heard arguments and then failed to overturn legalized abortion. The timing and connection of these earthquakes are an awesome warning-judgment from God!

God's mercy is shown in the Landers quake. It occurred in an isolated area with very little damage and no loss of life occurred. An earthquake of this power in a heavily populated area would have caused tremendous damage. This earthquake seemed to showcase God's awesome power and timing. The quake was on the very morning of Gay Pride Day, and the Bible states God will destroy nations that practice open homosexuality.

God could have destroyed America on the morning of Gay Pride Day, June 28, 1992, with the Landers quake. This quake could have triggered the San Andreas fault and destroyed California. Those quakes that were triggered hundreds of miles away could have been 7.0 in power and destroyed huge sections of the West. More powerful quakes might have triggered the volcanoes to erupt. The entire western section of the nation could have been destroyed on the very morning of Gay Pride Day.

Think of the all the roads and bridges that would have been destroyed; the water aqueducts; the electric grids; the gas and oil pipelines; the railways; the food production; and industry. How would the injured be helped? The destruction would have thrown the nation into a tailspin. God in His mercy sent a warning. The Landers earthquake by itself is enough of a warning from God that awesome judgment is ahead. America has been warned!

March 1993

On March 18, 1993, the state of Oregon passed a Medicaid-rationing plan. This plan had twice before been passed by the state legislature; however, the federal government twice told Oregon that the law discriminated against the disabled. On both occasions, the plan was withdrawn. The plan called for ranking medical procedures by cost and benefits, and proposed not paying for procedures that were considered too costly or not beneficial.

The plan was criticized because it set up a "quality-of-life" standard and would deny medical treatment to people with treatable conditions. Pro-life people fought this legislation because it was laying the foundation for the possibility of euthanasia for the handicapped and terminally ill. This plan was also being set up as a model for other states and the federal government to follow. The Clinton Administration endorsed the plan, and it went into effect on February 2, 1994.

It is truly amazing that exactly one week after passing the Medicaid-rationing plan, on March 25, 1993, a 5.7 magnitude earthquake rocked the Pacific Northwest, but specifically Salem, Oregon, which is the state capital. Salem is not in an earthquake-prone area, so the earthquake came as a shock. What is truly ironic is the earthquake literally struck the state capital building and severely damaged the rotunda. The quake did very minor damage throughout the state; however, it severely damaged the capital building!

This building was the very location where just one week before, legislation was passed laying the foundation for euthanasia. This earthquake striking Salem one week after the passage of quality-of-life legislation was a clear warning. The very building where the legislation was passed was rocked and damaged by an earthquake that did little damage elsewhere.

No matter how much propaganda the supporters of the plan put forth, this plan set up a quality-of-life criteria for treating the sick. In the long term, there will be much death of the weak and innocent because of this legislation, and God was clearly warning America. This was a major step in promoting euthanasia.

Americans already disrespect life in the womb, as over 1.5 million "unwanted" babies are aborted every year. How long before Americans accept the use of euthanasia for "unwanted" parents or grandparents? This nation is now being set up to kill the unwanted sick and handicapped, and God has already forewarned.

June 1993

Gay Pride Day 1993 brought monumental judgment from God. During the late winter and entire spring of 1993, heavy rains fell on the Midwest. The Mississippi and Missouri rivers rose and approached flood stage. By mid-June the rivers were just at flood stage. On June 25, shipping was halted on the Mississippi River. As Gay Pride Day, **June 27, 1993**, approached, the rains increased until *USA Today* reported: "Then the skies opened up on June 19–21 filling the tributaries; and **on June 25–27, finally putting the rivers over their banks**." The Mississippi and Missouri rivers actually began flooding on the weekend of Gay Pride Day. The Great Flood of 1993, the worst in American history, started on Gay Pride Day. Literally, on **June 27, 1993**, as hundreds of thousands of homosexuals and their supporters paraded in American cities, the great rivers in the Midwest were overflowing their banks.

This flood turned out to be one of the greatest disasters in American history. The flood resulted in over $15 billion in damage; it destroyed 45,000 homes; 74,000 people had to be evacuated; two million acres were flooded; and hundreds of counties were affected. This was an awesome flood. What is so ironic is that after months of heavy rain, the actual date the rivers overflowed their banks was on the weekend of Gay Pride Day.

Gay Pride Day 1992 resulted in an awesome earthquake that shook the entire western area of the country, and Gay Pride Day 1993 was the start of the worst flood in American history, a flood that devastated the entire Midwest section of the country. The warnings are so clear—open and bold homosexuality is bringing the wrath of God on the nation.

July 1993

Gay Pride Day 1993 was followed in July by a nationwide attempt by Operation Rescue to save babies from being aborted. Operation Rescue coordinated the attempt to peacefully save babies in 10 cities throughout America. This attempt, called Cities of Refuge, took place July 9–18, 1993, and received national media attention. None of the Operation Rescue members were arrested for violence.

The Cities of Refuge event met well-planned resistance from the police and pro-abortion supporters. This resistance against Operation Rescue always has large numbers of militant homosexuals who mock our holy God. While members of Operation Rescue were praying in front of the abortion centers for the lives of unborn children, homosexuals and hard-core abortion supporters were mocking them and uttering blasphemous insults to God.

While this confrontation between good and evil was taking place in 10 of America's major cities, incredible rains fell on the Midwest. These rains of incredible strength actually began the same time as Cities of Refuge. The great rivers of the Midwest had been overflowing their banks since

June; however, even more intense rain began on July 9.

The *New York Times* reported the awesomeness of the storms that began on July 9 in an article titled "Flooded by Endless Rainfall, Midwest Braces for Still More." The article stated:

> Gushing rainfall in the Upper Midwest overnight was overwhelming dams and levees today and is threatening to unleash flooding not seen in more than a century: "We've never seen anything like this before," said Ron Fournier, a spokesman for the Army Corps of Engineers, noting that the rainfall is breaking records since records were kept in the early 1800s—"It's amazing;" "It's like water rising over the sides of a bathtub . . . there's not a dry spot in Iowa."

Rains up to eight or more inches a day fell on Iowa. Satellite photographs showed the flooding was so widespread in Iowa, the entire state looked like a new Great Lake!

Just after Operation Rescue ended, the Senate approved Ruth Bader Ginsburg, who is pro-abortion, as a justice to the Supreme Court. On July 22, 1993, five female senators made a pledge to allow abortion for millions of federal workers. While the Senate was approving Ginsburg and the senators were making their pledge, the torrential rains continued to fall. Soon after Operation Rescue and the pro-abortion political activity ended, the torrential rains stopped; however, it was weeks before the flood waters subsided.

The fierce opposition against saving unborn children, plus pro-abortion political activity, occurred during some of the worst rains in American history. These rains caused the worst flooding in American history. Scientists reported the rains and floods were so severe that they occur, on the average, only every 500 years. This disaster again coincided with homosexual and abortion-related events. The nation has again been warned that awesome judgment lies just ahead if the killing of God's children continues.

January 1994

On January 17, 1994, the Los Angeles area was rocked by a powerful 6.8 magnitude earthquake. The quake was centered in Northridge, about 25 miles from downtown Los Angeles. This powerful quake caused an estimated $25 billion in damage and caused widespread destruction. The quake was so powerful that it caused the Santa Susanna Mountains to rise one foot and the Los Angeles basin area to shrink. This was a massive move of a huge area of land.

What is extremely interesting about this earthquake is the fault which caused it was never identified. The location of the fault that caused the earthquake is a mystery to scientists. This powerful earthquake . . . just happened. The scientists also found this earthquake was like two separate quakes. The first movement was a powerful upward thrust of the earth followed by a violent shaking of the earth. The upward thrust was so powerful that it lifted buildings off their foundations. Scientists described this earthquake as having a "one-two punch."

This quake occurred one day after Sanctity of Life Sunday and five days before the twenty-first anniversary of *Roe v. Wade*, the Supreme Court decision which legalized abortion. Sanctity of Life Sunday began in 1984 and occurs the Sunday before the anniversary of *Roe v. Wade*. On January 16, 1994, over 50,000 churches in America were praying to end abortion.

Southern California is one of the abortion centers of the nation. Over 310,000 babies are aborted ever year in California; however the majority are aborted in southern California. The number of babies that have been legally killed in southern California is incalculable.

The epicenter of the quake was Northridge, which happens to also be the pornography center of America. Over 80 percent of all video pornography was made in the Northridge area. The earthquake literally destroyed the pornography industry in Northridge, as the entire pornography center was within five miles of the epicenter. Pornography is one of the top 100 industries in California.

A survey after the earthquake reported that every pornography maker in the area had been damaged. The pornography industry was hit so hard by the quake that Lenny Friedlander, president of a large pornography business, was reported by the Associated Press as saying, "These religious fanatics may think it's the Lord's way of telling us, Hey straighten your act out." The quake also closed nine abortion centers, including Her Medical Clinic in Pacoima. This abortion center reportedly kills 80 to 120 babies every Saturday, and advertised to abort babies up to 28 weeks.

One day after Sanctity of Life Sunday and five days before the anniversary to legalize abortion, the pornography center and a major abortion center of America were rocked by a powerful earthquake! This earthquake closely fits the description that the Bible gives for judgment on a nation for child killing and sexual immorality: "The land is defiled: therefore I do visit the iniquity thereof upon it, and **the land itself vomiteth out her inhabitants**" (Lev. 18:25).

The violent upward thrust of the land, directly under Northridge, gives the clear symbolic picture of the land vomiting out its inhabitants. It is almost as if the land could not tolerate anymore the pornography and innocent shed blood on it. With this earthquake, it seems so fitting the land was vomiting out its inhabitants—it is eerie. God was again very merciful because the loss of life was very low. The warning–judgments are so clear and are getting increasingly awesome.

To put God's earthquake-warnings into perspective— since October 1989 seven major earthquakes (6.3 or greater magnitude) have hit California. These earthquakes have all occurred on or very near to major abortion and/or homosexual related events. Six of the earthquakes have taken place since April 1992!!! God has been very merciful because most of the quakes were centered in remote areas, or if the quake hit a populated area, the loss of life was light; thus they serve as awesome warning-judgments.

March 1994

In March, several hundred members of Operation Rescue attempted to save babies from being aborted in Birmingham, Alabama. The event, titled Holy Week Passion for Life, took place between March 25 and April 3. This event was totally nonviolent; however, approximately 200 demonstrators were arrested for praying on the sidewalk in front of the abortion centers. No arrests were made for violence. The militant pro-abortion supporters, including homosexuals and lesbians, were present as "clinic defenders," to insure the abortion centers stayed open. They wanted to insure that the babies would continue to be killed. The lesbians and homosexuals made up a large percentage of the "clinic defenders."

The homosexuals and lesbians, while they were guarding the doors to the abortion centers, made profane statements against our holy God. A group of ministers from various religious backgrounds and denominations even held a news conference to voice their support for the Emergency Coalition for Choice. This coalition was organized to insure the abortion centers were kept open during the protest. On March 27, two days after Holy Week Passion for Life began, a series of violent and destructive thunderstorms and powerful tornadoes roared across Alabama and then the South causing death and awesome destruction.

The storms then spread to Georgia and North and South Carolina killing dozens of people. A spokesman for the National Weather Service in Birmingham described the tornadoes as, "One of the worst ones I've seen, one of the worst ones this century." The tornadoes were characterized as F4, which means the winds were between 207 and 260 mph These are awesome tornadoes. It is interesting to note that the tornadoes destroyed three churches.

USA Today printed a map of the areas hit by the storm with the heading "Route of Killer Storm." The map illustrated that the tornadoes first touched down in north central Alabama, the Birmingham area, and then spread to the other states.

The worst tornadoes this century touching down near Birmingham during an attempt to save innocent life in the womb was no coincidence. You can almost see the anger in our holy God as the attempt to save the babies meets fierce resistance from militant homosexuals and pro-abortion supporters. The power of the government was also used to insure that the abortion centers were kept open. These confrontations at the abortion centers seem to highlight how angry God is over the killing of His children in the womb.

With God there is no such thing as an unwanted child. All children are precious to Him: "Lo, children are an heritage of the Lord; and the fruit of the womb is his reward" (Ps. 127:3).

June 1994

During the spring, many economists were predicting the growth of the economy would cause the stock market to surge to record heights. They were predicting that the stock market would rise dramatically during the summer. On June 17, the dollar's value suddenly began to plunge against the German and Japanese currencies. The plunge continued until early July when the dollar began to stabilize at record lows.

The stock market soon followed the dollar and began

to fall. During the week of June 19, the market lost 187 points, or 4.7 percent of its value. The newspapers had headlines such as "Stock Market Reels," "Dollar Plunges Worldwide Threatening U.S. Recovery," "Dollar Puts Summer Rally in Deep Freeze," and "Dollar's Slide Could Hamstring Economy." The economists who were so optimistic were now stunned. It is very noteworthy that the plunge in the dollar came as a shock. The economists were baffled as to why the dollar started to collapse.

Coinciding exactly with the dollar's plunge was Gay Pride Week and the Gay Olympic Games in New York City. The week ended with Gay Pride Day. The Gay Games took place between June 18 and 25, ending with Gay Pride Day on the June 26.

The *New York Times* reported that 11,000 athletes participated in the games, and between 500,000 and one million attended the games. The Gay Games were even sponsored by corporations like AT&T. Gay Pride Day ended with a huge parade on New York City's Fifth Avenue. There are reports that hundreds or possibly thousands of homosexuals marched naked on Fifth Avenue.

It is no coincidence that the dollar began to plunge on June 17—the very start of Gay Pride Week. New York City is the financial capital of the United States, if not the world. The dollar is the basis of the United States economy and many foreign currencies are also tied to the dollar. The best way for God to get the attention of the entire nation is by touching the economy.

Immediately after Gay Pride Day, the dollar stabilized and the stock market began to recover. The stock market then began to recover its loss and started an upward advance toward new highs. The exact time of Gay Pride Week interrupted the upward climb of the market. The plunge of the value of the dollar during Gay Pride Week remains as the dollar's all time low.

The American economy was shaken mightily during Gay Pride Week and the Gay Olympic Games. Homosexuals marching boldly through the streets of New York City did not go unnoticed by our holy God. What more does God have to do to get American's attention that open and bold homosexuality is bringing awesome judgment on the nation? The huge homosexual march in Washington, D.C., on October 11, 1987, was followed eight days later by one of the greatest stock market crashes in American history. The warning of awesome economic judgment could not be any clearer.

A review of these Gay Pride Days reveals the clear pattern of judgment from our holy God. On June 28, 1992, the very morning of Gay Pride Day, two huge earthquakes shook the entire western section of the country. One quake registered 7.6 and was the fourth most powerful quake to hit America this century. On Gay Pride Day, June 27, 1993, the Great Flood of '93 began. After weeks of heavy rain, the great rivers of the Midwest actually began to overflow their banks on the weekend of Gay Pride Day. As the homosexuals were preparing for Gay Pride Day and then marching down the streets of American cities, the greatest flood in U.S. history was literally beginning.

The powerful earthquakes on Gay Pride Day 1992 shook the entire western section of the country. The floods of 1993 affected the entire Midwestern section of the country. Gay Pride Day 1994 affected the entire nation as Wall Street and the economy were shaken mightily. What judgment will future Gay Pride Days bring on America? America is on a direct collision course with God over open and bold homosexuality.

July 1994

The correlation between the attack on those who attempt to save babies from being aborted and awesome disasters continued in July 1994. An attempt was made by pro-life demonstrators on July 6–9 to save babies in Little Rock, Arkansas. As usual, the police and "clinic defenders" were on hand to insure the abortion centers stayed open and the babies were killed. The homosexuals and lesbians again made up a large percentage of the "clinic defenders." Ministers from various religious backgrounds and denominations came out to publicly support abortion.

On July 6, coinciding exactly with the attempt to save babies, Tropical Storm Alberto stalled over western Georgia, including the Atlanta area. In one day alone, Alberto dumped 21 inches of rain. Torrential rains lasted during the exact time period of the protest and then stopped. The state of Georgia was in shock over the storm's suddenness and the resulting flood destruction. Thousands were left homeless, and hundreds of thousands of people were without water. The floods caused hundreds of millions of dollars in damage, and over 400,000 acres were flooded. The storm was called the worst in over a century to hit the state. The scientists referred to Alberto as the type of storm that hits an area only once every 500 years.

The state of Georgia has been particularly brutal to anyone trying to save babies in the womb. Atlanta police have been especially hard on peaceful pro-life demonstrators. In one instance, Christians were thrown in jail for 18 days for praying on a sidewalk in front of an abortion center. The police conduct had been so outrageous against pro-life demonstrators that in 1993 a federal judge awarded them $37,500 in damages. The judge also required the police to take special training in how to deal with protesters. Several years ago, the attorney general for Georgia boasted that, if necessary, he would build detention camps big enough to hold all the pro-life activists who protested in front of abortion centers.

How ironic, that at the exact time Christians are praying and trying to save babies in the womb, an area of the country that has been so hostile to the saving of the babies suffers the worst flood in over a century. The timing of the events and the history of the state of Georgia's and the city of Atlanta's hostility toward life make this seem as God's retribution.

September 1994

During September, Vice-President Al Gore represented the United States at the World Population Control Conference in Cairo, Egypt. As expected, he promoted abortion as a method of birth control. Abortion was promoted as a universal right. Gore's ideas were vigorously opposed by several countries and many religious leaders.

On September 12, the next to the last day of the conference, a powerful 6.3 magnitude earthquake rocked southern California. This was the eleventh most powerful earthquake this century to hit the United States. This earthquake was, again, in an isolated area and very little damage was done. The timing of this earthquake again connects with an abortion-related event.

One has to wonder: What would have happened if Vice-President Gore had his way at the Cairo conference? Maybe this earthquake would have been 8.0 or greater magnitude and caused awesome damage. The timing of the earthquake with the Cairo conference was not a coincidence, but this is yet another in a series of God's warnings. God has given America so many warnings!

October 1994

In October, a tropical storm stalled over southwestern Texas and in three days up to 30 inches of rain fell. The Houston area was particularly hit hard with flooding. In fact, the situation was very similar to the Georgia rains and floods earlier in the year. This was again the type of storm that occurs once every 500 years. There were no abortion or homosexual related events taking place while the rains fell.

What is interesting about Houston is that the city is just like Atlanta in its vehement hatred for those who try to peacefully defend babies in the womb. During August 1992, while the Republican Convention was being held in Houston, Christians peacefully protested and attempted to save babies. In Houston, Judge Eileen O'Neill declared a 100-foot non-demonstration zone around the city's 31 abortion centers. This was done at the request of the abortion centers and the **attorney general of the state of Texas**. Judge O'Neill issued an injunction against demonstrations. **She included prayer and Bible reading in her definition of a demonstration!** Several were arrested and held in jail without being charged with any crime. Finally, a *Writ of Habeas Corpus* was obtained from the State Supreme Court ordering the release of the pro-life demonstrators; they were released. A *Writ of Habeas Corpus* is used as a protection against illegal imprisonment. When was the last time in America a *Writ of Habeas Corpus* was needed to release peaceful protesters?

In May 1994, a Texas jury ordered the protesters involved in the 1992 incident to pay $204,585 to Planned Parenthood of Southeast Texas. Planned Parenthood said it incurred these expenses while trying to keep its Houston abortion center open during the protest. The jury also awarded Planned Parenthood and nine other abortion centers over $1 million in punitive damages. Nationwide, Planned Parenthood's abortion centers kill over 120,000 babies a year. This is by far the most babies killed by any one organization. How many babies have been killed by Planned Parenthood since abortion was legalized in 1973?

Both Houston and Atlanta are very similar in their efforts to destroy any attempt to save the lives of unborn babies. It is no coincidence that both cities were hit within four months of each other by tropical storms that dropped incredible amounts of rain, causing extensive damage. These storms are not hitting cities by coincidence; the shedding of innocent blood has begun to draw the wrath of God.

Americans have not supported Operation Rescue's efforts to peacefully save babies from being aborted, but the organized resistance against it has brought an awesome response from our holy God.

November 1994
In November 1994, a political earthquake of historic proportions shook American politics. For the first time in 40 years, the Republicans gained control of both the House of Representatives and the United States Senate. The Republican Party also gained several governorships and state legislatures around the country. For the first time since the Civil War, the Speaker of the House was not reelected. This election was of great importance in thwarting evil in America.

The Democratic Party had become the power base for the pro-abortion and homosexual rights agenda. There are several politicians in the Republican Party who also are pro-abortion, but the platform of the party is pro-life. Both Presidents Reagan and Bush were pro-life, and both appointed Supreme Court judges who were pro-life.

There are many Democrats who are pro-life (such as Robert Casey, the former governor of Pennsylvania); however, the party at large takes a militant, pro-abortion position and supports "homosexual rights." The party's platform is pro-abortion. President Clinton appointed pro–abortion justices to the Supreme Court. Shortly after taking office, he issued Executive Orders to overturn pro-life policies. He even tried to force the military to accept homosexuals. There are a few Democratic congressmen who are openly homosexual and are pushing the homosexual agenda. The Surgeon General was militant in pushing abortion and "homosexual rights." The very sins for which God's Word promises will bring His wrath on a country have found a home in the Democratic Party (not forgetting there are also Republicans who support these sins).

The election resulted in 40 pro-life congressmen and senators being elected. Not one pro-life incumbent congressman or senator lost to a pro-abortion challenger. The long-term grip of pro-abortion politicians also has been broken. It seems that God has moved and given America one more chance to establish righteousness in the nation. There may not be much time, and this may be the last political opportunity God will provide. Does America have the moral base to stop the homosexual rights agenda and the legal killing of God's children in the womb? God has been extremely merciful and provided the political base to stop these sins. Does America have the moral foundation to change from its collision course with God? Ultimately, the politicians reflect the will of the people. If Americans do not have the will, the nation will continue on the collision course.

In November 1994, Tropical Storm Gordon tore through Florida, causing hundreds of millions of dollars in damage to the winter vegetable crop. The storm dropped record rains over Florida, destroying over 35,000 acres of crops. No abortion or homosexual-related activities were taking place during this time. It is interesting that during 1994, three tropical storms suddenly arose and did incredible damage to the states of Florida, Georgia, and Texas. Two of the states are the homes of large cities which have a long record of rejecting any attempt to save the lives of innocent babies in the womb.

January 1995
A series of powerful storms struck the entire state of California and lasted through March. From the Oregon state

line to Mexico, awesome rain storms wrecked havoc in 40 of California's 58 counties. The storms caused enormous flooding, and they even created some tornadoes. The rains and flooding resulted in 39 counties being declared disaster areas. The total destruction reached $2 billion. These storms were the type scientists identified as occurring once every 500 years.

These floods are one in a series of disasters which have struck California since the San Francisco earthquake of October 1989. Since 1989, California has suffered through the worst fires, floods, mud slides, riots, economic depression, municipal government bankruptcy, and destructive earthquakes in its history. In six years the disasters have resulted in more than $32 billion in damage. These disasters are hitting the state that produces 80 percent of the nation's pornography; aborts over 300,000 babies a year; has two cities with some of the largest homosexual populations in the world; has Hollywood, which produces vile movies (it is known for fornication and adultery); and has a tremendously violent crime rate. All these bring the wrath of God.

It seems that God has a death grip on the state. When comparing California and the current disasters with the Bible, one verse seems appropriate: "He turneth rivers into a wilderness, and the watersprings into a dry ground; a fruitful land into barrenness, for the wickedness of them that dwell therein" (Ps. 107:33–34). This once beautiful and blessed state is slowly being turned into a continually cursed land.

April 1995

Operation Rescue targeted New Orleans, Louisiana, for its annual Easter prayer and protest. This event was titled Holy Week Passion for Life and took place between April 10 and 16.

New Orleans was labeled the murder capital of America because, per capita, it had the highest murder rate of all the nation's cities. During 1994, 421 people were murdered in the city. Prior to April 10, there had been 115 murders, which was more than seven per week.

The leaders of Operation Rescue led prayer meetings in front of the city's abortion centers and publicly asked God to control the murdering spirit in New Orleans. Because of the prayer meetings, the abortion centers closed for the week. To the amazement of everyone, not one murder occurred in the city between April 10 and 16. This occurred even with 120 to 200 police officers being taken off the streets and used to protect the abortion centers. The media even reported that there were no murders in the city during the Holy Week Passion for Life. The yearly murder rate statistics for New Orleans were way down. The high murder rate was broken during the Holy Week Passion for Life. The drop in the murder rate corresponded exactly with the closing of the abortion centers!!!

Research by Operation Rescue has shown that other cities were blessed like New Orleans by the presence of Operation Rescue and the closing of the abortion centers. The murder and violent crime rate plummeted during the time of Operation Rescue's presence, prayer, and protest. (The connection between killing children in the womb and crime in America is covered in chapter four.)

During the Holy Week Passion for Life, pro-abortion supporters would defend the abortion centers. They continued the vile mocking of God and were supported by large numbers of homosexuals and lesbians. On April 14 (Good Friday), a powerful 5.6 magnitude earthquake jolted Texas and New Mexico. This was the most powerful earthquake in this section of the country in 75 years. The quake was centered in a sparsely populated area of Texas, and there was very little damage. During the height of the Holy Week

Passion for Life and the intense mocking of God by pro-abortion supporters, two states were rocked by a powerful earthquake.

God did two things during the Holy Week Passion for Life. He blessed New Orleans by breaking the murderous spirit over the city; however, at the same time, a clear warning was given to the nation by the powerful earthquake shaking two very large states!

August–October 1995

The year turned out to be a record for the most hurricanes and tropical storms. The 1995 hurricane season was the second busiest in 125 years of record keeping. There were 19 named storms for this year. Although there were 19 storms, only two hit the United States. Hurricane Erin hit the Florida panhandle on August 3, while Hurricane Opal also hit the Florida panhandle on October 4.

The timing of these two hurricanes hitting the country was in direct connection to abortion related issues. In late

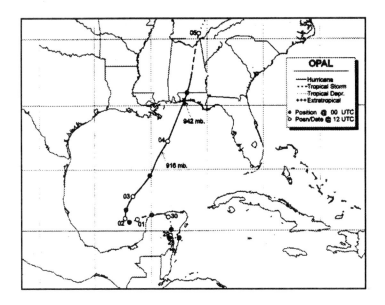

July and early August pro-life congressmen tried to prevent Planned Parenthood from receiving $193 million in federal funds. Planned Parenthood is the largest abortion organization in the United States. It has abortion centers throughout the United States, and these centers are responsible for killing more than 120,000 babies every year.

The battle to block the funding obtained national significance and was reported by the national media. On August 2 the battle was lost, and the funding for Planned Parenthood was approved. On this same day, Tropical Storm Erin tore through central Florida and entered into the Gulf of Mexico. The storm gained strength over the Gulf and developed into a hurricane. Hurricane Erin turned north, and on August 3, it slammed into the Florida panhandle.

On Saturday, September 30, 1995, Hurricane Opal entered the Gulf of Mexico and headed in a very slow easterly direction. Opal was classified as a Category 3 in power. The course of the hurricane was parallel to the United States, but headed directly toward Mexico. On October 2, around 11 a.m. (Eastern Standard Time) the hurricane suddenly changed direction. The storm made a sharp 90–degree turn, began to strengthen in intensity, accelerated in speed, and headed directly for the Florida panhandle. (See map which tracked the storm.) It was as if an unseen force just pulled this powerful hurricane off course toward the United States. Hurricane Opal hit on October 5, very near the same location as Erin.

What is truly amazing is that on October 2, the Supreme Court of the United States made a pro-abortion ruling. The court refused to hear a challenge to the Freedom of Access to Clinic Entrances Act (FACE) law. The FACE law was created to limit pro-life protest at the abortion centers and has become a powerful tool against peaceful pro-life protesters. The law was challenged as being unconstitutional. The court refused to hear the challenge and let the law stay intact. This became a major pro-abortion victory.

Although Hurricane Opal hit the United States three days after the Supreme Court's decision, the hurricane actually changed course around the time of the decision. **It is quite possible that at the very time the Supreme Court made the announcement it had refused to hear the challenge to the FACE law, Hurricane Opal changed direction, accelerated, and headed directly at the United States.** Opal was a large, powerful storm that pounded 120 miles of the Florida coast. It hit with winds of 140 mph and caused $3 billion in damage. Opal became the third most destructive hurricane to hit the United States.

January 1996

The winter of 1996 proved to be one of the worst on record and surpassed the winter of 1994 in severity. Record cold temperatures with a wind chill of 90 degrees below zero hit many Midwestern states. Entire states were paralyzed by the cold and snow. Record snow fell on the East Coast, and the "blizzard of the century" hit in mid-January. The cold and snow were so severe in Pennsylvania that the governor closed the state's roads for two days. The winters of 1994 and 1996 were the two worst since the 1880s when records were started.

On January 19, a thaw and warm rain fell on Pennsylvania, and the snow and ice began to melt. On the January 20, the rivers began to flood, and thus began the worst flooding in two decades. Two days later was the twenty-third anniversary of the Supreme Court decision *Roe v. Wade.* Also on January 22, the court made a pro-abortion decision regarding Pennsylvania. The court upheld a lower court's ruling that the state's strict laws regarding Medicaid–funded abortions were unfair, and the laws were stricken.

It was amazing to see the Pennsylvania newspapers on

January 22 and 23 with headlines such as "River of death," "Flooding worst since '72," "Flooding effect crushing," together with abortion related headlines, "State loses appeal on abortion, Stricter-than-U.S. rule barred in Pennsylvania." When reading the newspapers, it was so simple to visually associate the flooding and the abortion decision.

Pennsylvania had just experienced the "blizzard of the century" and the worst flooding in 20 years, and at the exact time the Supreme Court made a pro-abortion ruling regarding the state. Could all this just be another coincidence? On January 22, the connection between a pro–abortion Supreme Court decision and awesome destruction was so clear. The connection could not be missed by anyone who truly feared God. The newspaper's headlines made the connection for you!

March 1996

On March 8, the stock market plunged 171 points in one day. This plunge at this time was the third greatest one-day plunge in history. The bond market also plunged on this day. The entire financial market was shaken. The plunge made headlines on all the nation's newspapers and radio reports.

When trying to analyze the plunge, all the experts were mystified for an explanation. A very good report on the job market was released by the Department of Labor and suddenly fear gripped all the financial markets that triggered a huge sell-off. There really was no explanation for the plunge in the market other than sudden fear gripped the entire market. Before the plunge, the market was near a record high. In the days that followed, the market recovered the loss and went on to record levels. This one-day plunge just stood out as a very strange event.

What also occurred on March 8, was a Michigan jury acquitted Dr. Jack Kevorkian, "Dr. Death," of assisting in two suicides of terminally ill people. Since 1990, Kevorkian had assisted 27 people in committing suicide. Just two days before the acquittal, a federal appeals court in San Francisco overturned a Washington state law that made physician–assisted suicide a felony. The nation was moving in the direction of allowing physicians to kill terminally ill patients. After being acquitted, Kevorkian said he was going to California to set up euthanasia centers.

Just as legalizing abortion opened the door for the slaughter of millions of innocent children in the womb, so could legalizing euthanasia open the door to killing thousands of grandmas and grandpas, moms and dads, mentally and physically handicapped, and others who are no longer "wanted."

America is moving into another area where more innocent blood will be shed. This will cause more of God's wrath to fall on the nation. The German Nazis started their extermination of millions of people by first giving the medical profession the right to euthanize the feebleminded, etc. The doctors in America already have a hardness toward killing as the profession aborts 1.5 million babies a year. America is moving into dangerous ground by allowing the medical profession to start killing patients. The Bible clearly states, "Thou shalt not kill."

The stock market plunge coincided exactly with the acquittal of Kevorkian. The *Washington Post* had the plunge and acquittal on the front page. The radio news reports had the acquittal and plunge as back-to-back stories. Will legalizing euthanasia accelerate God's awesome judgments on America? It seems with the unexplained stock market plunge, God has sent another warning that the shedding of innocent blood will bring his judgment.

May 1996
On May 20, 1996, the headlines of the *New York Times* read,

"Worst Drought Since '30s Grips Plains," and "Wheat Farmers and Ranchers Are Ruined." The article went on to report how a powerful drought had gripped the Midwest and western sections of the country. The states which were the hardest hit included Nebraska, Oklahoma, Texas, New Mexico, Arizona, and parts of California. The drought was so severe that tens of thousands of farmers were in danger of losing their farms, and the area was beginning to look like the Dust Bowl of the 1930s. The article pinpointed **October 1995** as when the drought started. The following quotes from the article shows the severity and effect of the drought:

> Since last October, an average of 2.32 inches of rain has fallen on the wheat fields and cattle ranches that dominate the landscape here in the Oklahoma Panhandle —the second driest period since the Oklahoma Climatological Survey started keeping records 101 years ago.
>
> From Kansas south to Texas, one of the worst droughts on record has pushed thousands of farmers on the Great Plains to the edge of financial ruin and spurred panic selling of cattle in some states.

The record-breaking drought was followed by record breaking heat. The article reported, "In parts of the Texas and Oklahoma panhandles, temperatures reached 105 degrees this week, the earliest that such temperatures have ever been recorded." This drought has the potential to literally turn huge sections of the country into dust!

Officials in Texas reported that the drought could cost the state $6.5 billion in agriculture losses, and as of May, the state already lost $2.4 billion. The agriculture commissioner of Texas said the drought had the potential to be the worst natural disaster in the twentieth century in Texas. The drought and severe winter caused the entire winter wheat crop to fail. The corn and soybean crops were also heavily damaged. If the drought had continued into 1997, America could have suffered severe food shortages with skyrocketing prices. Even when the drought lessened, tremendous damage had already been done.

October 1995 was pinpointed as the very start of the drought. **October 1995** was also designated as Gay/Lesbian History Month by the National Teachers Association (NEA). The NEA passed a resolution for every school district in the nation to observe October as Gay/Lesbian History Month. President Clinton, on October 20, announced his support for legislation that would bar job discrimination against homosexuals. He became the first president in history to support such legislation. The president's top advisor said that Clinton by supporting this legislation had "brought gay and lesbian issues out of the closet and into the open." The legislation was backed by 29 senators. Representative Barney Frank, who is a homosexual, said, "Clinton's endorsement of the legislation was of historic proportions."

One of the worst droughts this century started during Gay/Lesbian History Month! The very month the NEA tried to bring homosexuality into the nation's schools, the disastrous drought started. Could this drought be the beginning of God's judgment on the nation's food supply? The Bible states that before God judged Sodom and Gomorrah, the area was lush and well watered: "That it was well watered every where, before the Lord destroyed Sodom and Gomorrah, even as the garden of the Lord" (Gen. 13:10). Today this area is an arid wasteland where hardly anything lives or grows. Is this what is in store for America, if the nation continues to pursue the course of Sodom and Gomorrah!

The severity of the drought was first brought to the nation's attention with the *New York Times* headline article of May 20, "Worst Drought Since '30s Grips Plains." On the very next day, the United States Supreme Court overturned a section of Colorado's Constitution which prohibited special laws protecting homosexuality. With the headlines **"Worst Drought Since '30s Grips Plains"** fresh in mind, the headlines followed two days later with **"Gay Rights Laws Can't Be Banned High Court Rules."** The drought started during Gay History Month and came to the nation's attention almost to the day the Supreme Court made a landmark pro-homosexual decision!

July 1996

On July 12, 1996, Hurricane Bertha slammed into the North Carolina coast. Bertha was a moderate hurricane, packing winds up to 105 miles per hour, which resulted in nearly $200 million in damage. Hurricanes hitting North Carolina are not unusual, but a hurricane hitting the United States in July is extremely rare. Bertha was the first hurricane this century to hit the East Coast of the United States in July. All other hurricanes in July that approached the coast always turned northeast and out to sea. This was an extremely rare event.

At the exact moment Bertha slammed into North Carolina, the United States House of Representatives was debating the Defense of Marriage Act. The state of Hawaii was in the process of recognizing a "homosexual marriage" as equal to a heterosexual marriage for legal purposes. This is known as same-sex marriage. If Hawaii recognized a same-sex marriage, the Constitution of the United States would require the other states to also recognize this "marriage." Legislation was introduced to try and prevent the federal government from recognizing homosexual marriages and to prevent the states from being forced to recognize such marriages as being legal. The House voted to pass the act by a vote of 342 to 67.

While the House overwhelming voted to pass the act,

the Defense of Marriage Act shows just how degenerate America has become. Legislation is now needed to define and protect the institution of marriage! The homosexual agenda is working state by state, and they will not rest until homosexuality is legally recognized in the entire country. Several states allow homosexuals to adopt children, and several major cities legally recognize homosexual partners for spousal benefits. Some major corporations such as AT&T and Disney already provide benefits for homosexual partners. America is a long way down the road toward recognizing same-sex marriages.

The stock market was in chaos during the time of this debate. The day before the debate, the market dropped 83 points; the day of the debate, it dropped 10 points; and the day after, it dropped 161 points. This drop was up to this time the fourth greatest one-day drop in history. The total drop for the three days was 259 points. The stock market plunge frightened investors, and billions of dollars were withdrawn. The plunge literally rocked the stock market.

At the exact time the House was debating the Defense of Marriage Act, an extremely rare hurricane slammed into the United States, resulting in $200 million in damage. Coinciding with the debate, the stock market plunged 259 points. The day after the debate, the stock market plunged 161 points for the fourth greatest plunge in history. This is just another in a long series of warnings God has given America.

An extremely rare hurricane and a huge stock market plunge occurring during the debate over same-sex marriage is God's way of trying to get the national attention of America. God created the institution of heterosexual marriage, and it is clear that He intends to defend it.

September 1996
Early in September, powerful Hurricane Fran, a large and

powerful storm, headed toward the United States. The storm was so powerful that it was compared to Hurricane Hugo. Fran was classified as a Category 3 in power. Over 500,000 people were evacuated from the coast in South Carolina alone. Fran smashed into North Carolina on the evening of September 5, with 115 mph winds, causing over $1 billion in damage. On September 5, the United States Senate debated the Defense of Marriage Act. This act was to outlaw same-sex marriages. The Senate eventually passed the act.

The very day of the debate, this powerful hurricane smashed into North Carolina. In July 1996, while the United States House of Representatives debated this act, Hurricane Bertha also smashed into North Carolina.

Governor Jim Hunt said of Hurricane Fran, "This is devastation like we have never seen." The hurricane did over $1 billion in damage. Fran destroyed huge sections of North Carolina's agriculture. The storm brought record flooding to West Virginia, and ironically, sections of Washington, D.C., were flooded by the Potomac River. The hurricane hit while the Defense of Marriage Act was being debated, just as Hurricane Bertha hit in July as the House was debating the same act!

March 1997

On February 25, the Senate passed legislation to release $385 million overseas into 100 counties for "family planning." Pro-life forces in the Senate tried to stop the release of the funds because some of the money could be used for abortion. The Clinton Administration backed this release of funds and pushed the date of release of the funds to March 1.

On March 1, 1997, President Clinton signed the legislation into law, and the money was released. On the very next day, March 2, powerful tornadoes roared across Texas into Arkansas, Mississippi, Tennessee, and Kentucky. The storm stalled over Ohio, and torrential rains fell over Ohio causing record flooding on the Ohio River.

The tornadoes were so powerful, they were compared to Palm Sunday storms of March 27–28, 1994. This storm in 1994 also hit directly on an abortion-related event and is reported in this book. The storm that hit Arkansas was so powerful that Governor Huckabee described the damage as of "apocalyptic proportions." The tornadoes actually destroyed the small town of Arkadelphia, Arkansas. Police Chief Bob Johnson said one tornado was 10 blocks wide. Arkansas Emergency Services reported, "These types of casualty figures are pretty much unprecedented here. It's a major disaster."

The storm caused record flooding along the Ohio River. The town of Falmouth, Kentucky, was nearly totally destroyed by the flooding. The flooding along the Ohio lasted for several weeks, causing extensive damage. This storm was identified as one which occurs every 500 years.

What is truly ironic is that President Clinton signed the legislation on March 1, which released the "family planning" money overseas. The very next day he signed disaster declaration legislation for nine counties in his own home state!

July 1997

From July 13 to July 19, 1997, Operation Rescue held a national prayer vigil in front of the abortion center of Doctor Martin Haskell of Kettering, Ohio. Dr. Haskell is credited with inventing the partial-birth abortion technique. On July 18, I traveled with Cops for Christ to participate in the prayer vigil. While driving to the abortion center, we discussed the possibility of God's judgment occurring during this Operation Rescue event.

The week was very quiet, with no great disasters occurring. We arrived late at night in Kettering. I went to bed and woke up the next morning, and to my astonishment found that overnight, Hurricane Danny had formed in the Gulf of Mexico. The hurricane was just sitting in the Gulf off the coast of Alabama. Danny was a small hurricane and finally moved inland. The storm dumped 30 inches of rain along the coast.

The strange thing about Danny is that it formed overnight in the Gulf of Mexico! When was the last time a hurricane just formed overnight in the Gulf? What a strange hurricane to develop during this national pro-life event! Every hurricane that has hit the United States since 1989 has been directly tied to abortion or homosexuality.

October 1997

On October 8, 1997, the United States Congress for the second time passed the partial-birth abortion ban. The House passed the ban by a veto-proof margin; however, it didn't pass the Senate by a veto-proof margin. When President Clinton vetoed the first legislation, there weren't enough votes in the Senate to overturn the veto. On October 10, the president quietly vetoed the partial-birth abortion ban.

In July 1997, an economic crisis began in Asia. By October, it began to affect the U.S. stock market. On October 6, the stock market began to lose ground. This began as the Congress was debating the partial-birth abortion ban. The loss in the stock market began to accelerate until it climaxed on October 27. On this day the market crashed a record 554 points, or about $600 billion. This was the greatest one-day point crash in history. During the period October 6–27, the market lost 13 percent and over $1 trillion.

The slide toward the greatest one-day stock market crash in history began during the partial-birth abortion debate and veto of the partial-birth abortion ban. If America continues to kill its children, it is crystal clear that God is going to destroy the nation's economy.

December 1997

On December 20, the headline across the nation's media was "New Early Abortion Technique." The technique was developed by Dr. Jerry Edwards, the medical director at Planned Parenthood in Houston, Texas. The procedure can be used on women eight to 10 days after conception. This information was the lead story on the national television nightly news. The story immediately following was the destruction in Texas by a powerful storm that developed in the Gulf of Mexico and roared into Texas.

This powerful storm with hurricane-force winds swept into Houston, doing tremendous damage. The entire state was pelted with snow, hail, rain, and hurricane-force winds. The news report actually focused on Houston, the very location where the new abortion technique was developed. It was amazing to see this news story about destruction in Houston following the abortion story which also was centered in Houston. The connection between abortion and judgment was neatly tied together by the nation's media. As one watched the news, it was impossible to miss!

January 1998

Bill Clinton was inaugurated as president on January 19, 1993. Three days later on January 22, the twentieth anniversary of *Roe v. Wade*, he signed documents which reversed years of restrictions on abortion. On January 22, 1993, Clinton reversed five abortion-related restrictions. The restrictions were: prohibition against abortion counseling in federally funded clinics; the ban on research on fetal tissue; the policy of abortion in the military; the ban to aid international family-planning programs which involve abortion; and he called for the review of the French abortion drug RU-486. He also would veto the partial-birth abortion ban twice. Clinton has done everything possible to protect and promote abortion.

On January 21, 1998, on the very eve of *Roe v. Wade*, President Clinton was humiliated by a terrible sex scandal. The scandal broke on the eve of the twenty-fifth anniversary of *Roe v. Wade* and almost five years to the very day that he promoted the five abortion issues.

Because of this scandal, the legal action against the president continued until he appeared before a grand jury on August 17. After his grand jury appearance, the president addressed the nation and admitted he had lied under oath in January. On September 9, the report of the investigation of the president was sent to the House of Representatives for possible impeachment and removal from office. On October 8, 1998, the House of Representatives voted for an impeachment inquiry of President Clinton. On December 19, 1998, the House of Representatives passed two articles of impeachment against the president.

The timing of its revelation was awesome in connection to the president's pro-abortion position. The most pro-abortion president was accused of a sex scandal on the eve of the twenty-fifth anniversary of *Roe v. Wade*.

March 1998
On March 23, 1998, the United States Supreme Court refused to hear a partial-birth abortion case which had come before it. The case involved the state of Ohio and a law enacted by the state which banned partial-birth abortions. The federal courts had ruled the law "unconstitutional" and barred the enforcement of the law. Ohio appealed the ruling to the Supreme Court which then refused to hear the case.

By not hearing the case, the lower court's ruling was left standing. This meant that partial-birth abortion remained legal, and the helpless babies in the womb were offered no protection by the court.

I became aware of the court's decision by listening to

the news on the radio. The next day, I went to a newspaper store and had a copy of the *New York Times* in my hand. The Supreme Court's refusal not to hear the case was a front-page story. I looked at the article, but I couldn't read it. I was so upset, I left without buying the newspaper. As I stood looking at the paper, I said in my heart, "Lord perhaps judgment will not fall on our nation for this."

The court had refused to protect the babies, and it allowed the senseless slaughter to continue. With all the scientific evidence about the baby in the womb, not protecting them from being slaughtered in late term was inexcusable.

The very next day, two young boys, ages 13 and 11, opened fire on their school, killing four classmates and a teacher. Eleven others were wounded in the attack. The boys ambushed their classmates as they left the school during a fire drill. This event was a true national tragedy. When in the history of our nation had an 13- and 11-year-old done such a thing?

As I heard about the senseless killings, my mind flashed back to the day before and the Supreme Court's refusal to protect the innocent babies in the womb. The court had allowed senseless violence to continue and now senseless violence committed by mere youngsters had cast a pall over the entire nation. A spirit of murder has been loosed in our nation. Leviticus 18:25 says that God will judge a violent nation with violence: "Therefore I do visit the iniquity thereof upon it." It appears that on March 24, God's hand of protection was removed from the nation. The spirit of murder has now even reached 11-year-olds.

Who can explain why an 11-year-old would kill his classmates? Who can explain why the court would allow the barbaric partial-birth abortion technique to continue to be legal?

On March 24, 1998, the first person to legally die by

euthanasia took place in Oregon. An elderly woman dying of cancer was given a lethal dose of barbiturates. Will this open the flood gates to more innocent shed blood in our nation? In the near future, will thousands of grandmas and grandpas be killed by euthanasia?

In the space of two days: the Supreme Court refused to ban partial-birth abortions; two children killed four classmates a teacher, and wounded 11 others; and the first person died by legal euthanasia. All these events affected the entire nation, because the shedding of innocent blood brings the wrath of God on our country.

June 1998

The first weekend in June has become Gay Days at Disney World in Orlando, Florida. Starting in 1991, tens of thousands of homosexuals gather the first weekend in June in Disney World. This year's event started on June 3 and ran through June 7. The month of June has also been designated as Gay Awareness Month. The last Sunday of June has become Gay Pride Day.

The president of the United States sent a letter of congratulations for the Gay and Lesbian Pride Celebration, 1998 at Disney World. In the letter, the president stated:

> Our ideals and our history hold that the rights guaranteed us as Americans are inalienable. They are embedded in our Constitution and amplified over time by our courts and legislature, and I am bound by oath of office and the burden of history to reaffirm them. . . . And we stand to lose when any person is denied or forced out of a job because of sexual orientation.

The president was saying that homosexuality was a constitutional right!

A review of the Gay Days '98 schedule of events was amazing! On June 3 from nine p.m. to three a.m. was an event titled "Who's Your Daddy?" The description of the event follows:

> A Leather; Latex and Bondage Party . . . Featuring live flogging and spanking, dominatrix, masters and slaves . . . plus live piercing. Sponsored by Absolute Leather, B.D/S.M. Group of Florida

There was two events called "Seductive Dancing." There were male strippers and female impersonators. Gay Days ended on June 7 with a "Sunday Gospel Brunch" from 10:15 a.m. until 3:30 p.m., and an event titled "S.I.N Tonight, Repent Tomorrow"! The president of the United States sent a letter of congratulation for events like this!

On May 30, 1998, Operation Rescue began a week-long prayer and intercession in Orlando. They prayed in front of the city's abortion centers; they exposed child pornography being sold at Barnes and Nobles Bookstores; and they prayed in front of Disney World as the homosexuals entered. The city of Orlando flew the homosexual flag (the rainbow) on the flagpoles around City Hall. The flags remained up for the entire month of June. The Christians went to City Hall and warned of the danger with God by flying this flag. They were ignored. In fact, Operation Rescue received very little support from the churches in Florida. Operation Rescue ended the prayer vigil on June 6 at approximately 2:30 p.m.

At approximately 2:30 p.m. on June 6, fires erupted northeast, east, and southeast of Orlando and burned eastward, away from the city. There had been wildfires burning since May 25 (one week before Gay Month in Florida). These fires had been controlled and didn't receive national attention. At the very time Operation Rescue closed in prayer on June 6, the fires that started burned out of control for the entire month! For the rest of June fires burned all over Florida, but especially northeast of Orlando. In total there were over 2,000 fires and 500,000 acres burnt. With all the fires, only 300 houses were destroyed with no loss of life. The fires and drought caused over $1 billion damage in crop loss.

Gay Days ended in Disney World on June 7 with a "Gospel Brunch." On June 7, Florida governor Lawton Chiles declared a state of emergency because of the fires and mobilized the National Guard. The fires were burning totally out of control the very day that Gay Days ended! President Clinton issued a letter of congratulations to the homosexuals for Gay Days, and then just 12 days after it ended, he declared Florida a disaster area for the release of federal assistance. What irony.

The fires closed 130 miles of I-95, and 40,000 people were forced to evacuate their homes. A drought settled over Florida and huge amounts of crops were lost. The danger of the fires were so real that the governor even requested the citizens pray and ask God for rain. At the very height of the danger, when the fires could have merged into an unstoppable wall of fire miles long, the rains came. The state was spared, and on July 7 the people were allowed to go back home.

On June 30 the federal district court in Miami halted the enforcement of the state law banning the partial-birth abortion technique. This was at the height of the fire! This federal injunction occurred in conjunction with the worst fires in the state's history!

What an awesome warning to the state of Florida and the entire nation. Operation Rescue warned Orlando and Disney World of the dangers of open homosexuality and killing babies in the womb. They were rejected by Orlando. They were ignored by the entire state, but they warned of the possible judgment to come. Operation Rescue closed in prayer, and thus began the worst fires in the state's history. People that were too busy or did not care about the 100,000 homosexuals gathering in Orlando and the city flying the gay flag were now, a few days later, pleading with God for rain. They were fleeing their homes in panic as the fires threatened entire cities. This all occurred during Gay Month and while the homosexual flag was flying over one of the states largest cities.

God was merciful because there was no loss of life, and relative to the size of the fires, very few homes were lost. It is just amazing that the fires erupted as Operation Rescue ended in prayer, and while Gay Days was ending at Disney World the governor declared a state of emergency and mobilized the National Guard.

From this disaster, it is very evident that America is very close to eminent judgment from God. God's warning-judgments are coming to an end. The fires exploding right after Operation Rescue warned of judgment is no accident. The fires were a witness to Florida and the nation of the coming judgment for open and bold homosexuality and the killing of children in the womb.

The churches that prayed for rain, were they also interceding before God for the sin that is bringing judgment?

July 1998

On July 17, 1998, the stock market reached an all time record of 9,337 points. The following week the market began to plunge, and on July 23 it plunged 195 points for, up to this date, the sixth greatest one-day plunge ever. On July 23, the House of Representatives voted for a second time to override President Clinton's veto of the partial-birth abortion ban. On October 10, 1997, President Clinton had vetoed legislation which would have banned late-term abortions by the partial-birth technique. Starting on July 21, the House debated overriding the veto, and on July 23, voted overwhelmingly to override the veto. During this very week, the stock market plunged dramatically. The market fall continued into August until it fell 299 points on August 4. On August 31, the market fell 513 points for the second greatest one-day plunge in history. From the market high in July until August 31, the market plunged 1,800 points or about a 20 percent decline! In terms of dollars, $2 trillion was lost in six weeks.

At the very time the debate started in the House, the bottom literally fell out of the market, and it plunged wildly for weeks. On September 18, the Senate failed to override the president's veto of the partial-birth abortion ban.

Listening to the news on July 23 dramatically tied together abortion and disasters. The lead story of the day was President Clinton releasing $100 million in aid to drought-stricken Texas farmers; the story following was the vote by the House on overriding the partial-birth abortion ban veto; and following this story was the 195-point drop in the stock market. The articles followed each other, with abortion between the drought in Texas and the stock market fall! Even the national newspaper *USA Today* had all three events together on the front page!

August 1998

On August 10, San Francisco passed an ordinance to expand the city's "domestic partners" policy. The ordinance would require businesses in the city to offer domestic partners any customer discounts which are extended to married couples. The city was forcing businesses to recognize homosexual domestic partners as the equivalent to being married.

On August 12, a 5.4 magnitude earthquake rocked San Francisco. The quake was centered on the San Andreas fault. The earthquake occurred during the morning rush hour and disrupted traffic. The buildings in downtown San Francisco swayed, and the transit system was briefly shut down. There was very minor damage reported. Dozens of smaller quakes followed, and seismologists warned that this earthquake could be a warning of a greater one to come in the near future!

This earthquake occurred less than 48 hours after the ordinance was passed. It occurred right on the San Andreas fault. This is the fault which could level San Francisco and destroy entire sections of California. Has God put San Francisco on notice that tampering with His institution of marriage is going to bring awesome judgment to the city?

January 1999

Late on January 21 and into the early morning of January 22, a series of powerful tornadoes roared across Arkansas and then into Tennessee. This was a powerful storm that did over $1 billion in damage. This was a record-setting storm. The previous record for most tornadoes in one day in a state in January was 20; however, 38 hit Arkansas in less than 24 hours on January 21–22. The record for total tornadoes nationwide in January had been 52, but January 1999 witnessed 163. The majority fell in Arkansas and Tennessee.

The center of the storm was Little Rock, where tremendous damage occurred. The governor's mansion was in the direct path of the storm. Although the mansion was not damaged, several trees on the grounds were destroyed.

On January 21, ex-Senator Dale Bumpers of Arkansas spoke on behalf of President Clinton before the United States Senate. Senator Bumpers made a passionate speech to have the Senate dismiss the impeachment charges against the president. What was shocking with Bumpers' speech was he actually used the name of Jesus Christ on the floor of the Senate in a joke! Senator Bumpers told a story about an evangelist at a revival meeting. The evangelist asked a question, "Who has ever known anybody who even comes close to the perfection of our Lord and Savior, Jesus Christ?"

This question then lead into a joke. The purpose of this joke was to show that no one is perfect.

This use of the Lord's name was made by a man who twice supported the president's veto of the partial-birth abortion ban. He made the statement in front of the Senate which twice failed to overturn the president's veto of the partial-birth abortion ban. In addition, Bumpers had a nearly 100 percent pro-abortion voting record while he was a senator. How could this senator refer to Jesus Christ, as our Lord and Savior in front of this Senate!

Soon after the Bumpers' speech, this powerful storm tore into his home state and zeroed in on Little Rock. Meteorologists reported that it was one of the most unusual storms ever seen in January because it was strong and volatile. The storm triggered a phenomenon called "training," in which one tornado follows another like a freight train. The tornadoes came out of the sky in waves one after another. This storm generated 292 warnings during a 12-hour period beginning at 4:00 p.m. (EST). This was a record amount of warnings in the state for one storm. This was the second major storm to generate tornadoes in Arkansas in a week. This was the first time since records were started in 1878 that there were two storms in January that generated tornadoes. In many ways this was a record breaking storm.

January 22 was the twenty-sixth anniversary of *Roe v. Wade*, the Supreme Court decision which legalized abortion on demand. On this day, Hillary Clinton addressed the National Abortion Rights Action League (NARAL). She said that the president was going to seek $4.5 million from Congress to protect abortion centers. While Mrs. Clinton was making this speech, her home state was being declared a disaster area by the Federal Emergency Management Agency! The tornadoes that hit Little Rock literally tore down a tree on the governor's grounds which was called

Chelsea's tree. Chelsea is Clinton's daughter, and when the president was the governor of Arkansas, he had a tree house built for her. The tree which held her tree house was destroyed by these violent tornadoes. The destruction of Chelsea's tree received national attention. The headline from the Associated Press stated, "Twisters Rip South, Wreck Chelsea's Old Tree House."

From the time Senator Bumpers ended his speech defending the president until Hillary Clinton ended her pro-abortion speech, 48 tornadoes fell on America. Thirty-eight of them fell on Bumpers' and Clinton's home state. After hitting Arkansas, the tornadoes then hit Tennessee. The storm destroyed thousands of homes, left 100,000 homes without power, and did $1 billion in damage. The states of the most pro-abortion president and vice president were devastated on the anniversary of *Roe v. Wade*.

Apparently referring to Jesus Christ as our Lord and Savior on the floor of the Senate is something that should not be done lightly, especially by a senator who has done everything possible to promote abortion. The people of Arkansas elected both Bumpers and Clinton.

March 1999
Between March 21 and March 27, 1999, homosexual activists began a week-long campaign to promote same-sex marriage, homosexual adoption of children, and the passage of hate crime laws. The national campaign was called Equality Begins at Home (EBAH). It was sponsored by the National Gay and Lesbian Task Force and the Federation of Statewide Lesbian, Gay, Bisexual and Transgender Political Groups. This campaign included lobbying the 50 state legislatures with 300 separate activities in all 50 states. At least one state, Maryland, responded to this homosexual lobbying with pending legislation. On March 24 the Maryland House of Delegates gave approval to a law that would

ban discrimination based on sexual orientation. Governor Parris N. Glending had made this issue one of his top priorities.

On March 24, President Clinton authorized the attack on Serbia. The top military leaders in Russia made statements that World War III had begun. Vikto Chechevatov, a three-star general and commander of ground forces in Russia's Far East region, said this attack "was the beginning of World War III." Russia called for the draft of 200,000 soldiers. Russia mobilized its fleet and sent them into war maneuvers. During the maneuvers, Russia actually sent its bombers on a mock attack mission against America. The bombers were intercepted near Iceland and turned away from the route to America. Russia began to redeploy its tactical nuclear weapons. Russia had threatened NATO and America that the bombing of Serbia could lead to direct conflict with Russia.

On June 9, Serbia withdrew it forces from Kosovo and the tension over Serbia subsided. The effect of this attack on Serbia was that hostile relations developed between America and both Russia and China. The attack on Serbia has changed the entire course of world diplomacy. Russia and China have formed a military alliance to thwart the power of America. Russia has sold China advanced military weapons, and this alliance grows more powerful each month.

It is the opinion of this author that the attack on Serbia in the long run will be seen as a major change in the course of world history. This attack could lead to a major confrontation between America and both Russia and China in the months or years to come.

April 1999
On April 18, 1999, Operation Rescue began a week-long campaign called Operation Save America in western New

York. Although the campaign was located in western New York, it was a national event, as activists came from all over America to partake. Part of the campaign was to go to the high schools in the Buffalo-Rochester area with the gospel message of Christ. For several years, Operation Rescue has been going to high schools all over the country. Because the gospel of Jesus Christ is not allowed in the high schools, Operation Rescue members stand on the sidewalks in front of the schools and talk to the students.

Many cities have completely rejected Operation Rescue's attempt to reach high school students. For example, Operation Rescue members were arrested in Lynchburg, Virginia, and given a year in jail for standing on a sidewalk in front of a high school.

On April 19, 1999, Operation Rescue went to the high schools in western New York. The *New York Times* reported on April 20 that Operation Rescue had been to the high schools. On the evening of April 19, a prayer vigil was held. Operation Rescue's national director, Flip Benham, spoke about the violence in the nation's high schools. He talked about the violence that was going to be unleashed in the schools because America has rejected God. The very next day, high school students Eric Harris and Dylan Klebold attacked Columbine High School, in Littleton, Colorado, with bombs and guns.

This attack, without question, was the worst in our nation's history. A total of 15 died, and more than 20 were wounded in the assault. The killers sought out specific students to kill, and many of the students murdered were Christians. Some media have reported that a female student was asked by the killers if she believed in Jesus Christ just before they shot and killed her. In fact, between May 1998 and May 1999, approximately 10 high school students were killed because of their faith in Jesus Christ. In West Paducah, Kentucky, a Satanist killed four Christians at a school prayer meeting and wounded many others. High school students are now being martyred in America.

The attack on the students in Littleton occurred at the exact time Operation Rescue was being rejected at high schools in New York. The schools in New York are representative of all the schools across America! American schools are now closed to the gospel of Jesus Christ, and it appears that God is withdrawing His hand of protection. The Bible states, "The wicked shall be turned into hell, and all the nations that forget God" (Ps. 9:17). God is now on the outside of our schools and the devil is on the inside. America's schools are being turned into hell. Planned Parenthood, with its pro-abortion message, can come into our schools. Homosexuals, with their message, can come into the schools. Humanism and other godless ideology can be taught in the schools. The murdering spirit of killing babies in the womb has now infected our kids.

Immediately after the assault, schools all over America became the targets of violence. Students were arrested for planning attacks on the schools; the planning of killing teachers and students; and the bringing guns into school and setting off bombs. Is this now the future of America?

Fear has gripped many schools across America. To protect the students, many schools have been turned into fortresses with metal detectors and armed guards. The blessings of God have been removed, and the nation's schools are being turned into hell.

July 1999

During July, the worst drought during the twentieth century to hit New England and the mid-Atlantic states came into focus. By the end of July, it was the worst drought in 105 years of record-keeping to hit Delaware, Maryland, New Jersey, and Rhode Island. It was the second worst drought for Connecticut, New York, and West Virginia. The drought also severely affected Maine, New Hampshire, Pennsylvania, and Virginia. The total area affected by the drought was from Maine to Indiana and Kentucky to Virginia. The drought was so severe that even the Great Lakes fell to record lows.

The drought began in June 1998. According to the Climate Prediction Center, Washington, D.C., in June of 1998, the jet stream changed its course. The result of this change in the jet stream caused storms to go north or south of the drought area. Remember, June is now officially Gay Awareness Month. June was celebrated as Gay Awareness Month for several years. In June of 1999, the president of the United States signed a proclamation officially making June Gay Awareness Month. The president even designated the site of homosexual rioting in New York City in 1969 as a national historic site! The first stage of this record-setting drought took place in June 1998 during Gay Awareness Month with the change in the jet stream. During Gay Awareness Month 1999, the Northeast was experiencing the driest June on record!

The second stage of the drought took place during April, May, and June of 1999. During this time period, the driest weather ever recorded in 105 years of record keeping occurred. The rains literally stopped over most of New England and the mid-Atlantic. By mid-August all or parts of New Jersey, New York, Maryland, Connecticut, West Virginia, Rhode Island, Delaware, Pennsylvania, and Virginia were declared drought disaster areas. The drought caused over a billion dollars in crop losses. The epicenter of the drought became the state of Maryland.

The last week in March 1999 witnessed a huge homosexual political initiative called Equity Begins at Home (see March 1999 update for details of this event). During this initiative, the homosexuals lobbied all 50 state capitals for same-sex marriage, hate crime legislation, and the homosexual adoption of children. The state of Maryland was very receptive to this initiative and on March 23, 1999, passed legislation to ban discrimination against homosexuals. The *Washington Post* in a March 24, 1999, article titled "Md. House Likely to Pass Gay Rights Legislation" said that Governor Parris Glending had made homosexual rights one of his top priorities for 1999. On July 30, 1999, the *Washington Post* ran a front-page article titled "Md. Under Drought Emergency." The article said:

> **This year's** drought in Maryland is the second-worst since the government began keeping records in the 1880s. . . . Maryland has been among the hardest-hit drought areas in the nation.

The second stage of this awesome drought began immediately after the homosexual lobbying for same-sex marriage. Homosexual rights became the key issue for the state of Maryland and this state became the epicenter of the drought.

The drought began during Gay Awareness Month, and it accelerated **immediately** after the Equity Begins at Home initiative. The epicenter of the drought was Maryland, which made homosexual rights a top priority for 1999. The connection between the promotion of homosexuality and the worst drought in the state's history could not be any clearer.

To witness the continued correlation between homosexuality and this drought was awesome. On June 25, 1999, *USA Today* had an article titled "Record dry weather leaves farms parched." The article covered the drought in New England. One paragraph stated: "In **New England**, water levels already were low after a mild winter. But now, they're reaching danger levels under skies that remained mostly cloudless in April and May." In the very same newspaper, under the heading "Washington," subheading "Gay Rights," *USA Today* reported, "A bipartisan group of **New England** lawmakers unveiled a new version of legislation that would prohibit job discrimination against homosexuals." The states that were the center of the homosexual legislation were under tremendous drought.

August 1999

Along with Maryland, the state of New Jersey was the hardest hit by the drought. The drought virtually destroyed the entire state's agriculture. The drought began in June 1998 and after months of intensifying, finally on August 5, Governor Christie Whitman declared a drought emergency for the entire state. What is amazing about the declaration of the drought emergency is that the day before, August 4, the New Jersey Supreme Court made a pro-homosexual decision that made national headlines!

On August 4, 1999, the New Jersey Supreme Court ruled that the Boy Scouts of America could not bar homosexuals from the organization. This case received national attention and was the front-page story of the August 5 issue of *USA Today*. The article was titled "Court rejects ouster of gay Scout leader." The connection between homosexuality and the drought was made by the media for everyone to see. The very next day after the New Jersey Supreme Court made this pro-homosexual ruling, the entire state was declared a drought disaster area.

The nickname for New Jersey is the Garden State. The Bible states that God will turn a "garden" into a dry ground for the wickedness of those that dwell in it. This is exactly what happened to the Garden State. Psalm 107:33–34 reads, "He turneth . . . a fruitful land into barrenness, for the wickedness of them that dwell therein."

October 1999

On October 2, Governor Gray Davis of California signed into law several homosexual rights bills. One law officially recognized same-sex domestic partnerships and extended health insurance benefits to the unmarried partners of government employees. The signing of this law was set to coincide with a fund-raising banquet in Beverly Hills to honor President Clinton. This banquet was sponsored by Access Now for Gay Lesbian Equality.

On October 10, 1999, the California secretary of state chaptered these homosexual laws. On October 14, Governor Davis said, "For years America had looked to California to get a glimpse of the future. We've begun to offer leadership once again." Davis included in this "leadership for America" the recognition of homosexual domestic partnership. Davis wants all of America to follow California and recognize homosexual domestic partnership.

On October 16, the fifth most powerful earthquake to hit America in the twentieth century struck California. The earthquake, called Hector Mine, was 7.1 in magnitude and was located in the desert in a sparsely populated area. The earthquake did little damage, but shook three states. The earthquake was so powerful that it tore a 25-mile gash in the earth. Millions of people in California, Nevada, and Arizona felt the power of the quake. This quake triggered small quakes near the San Andreas fault, which was 120 miles away. Seismologists referred to this as "nerve-rattling conversation" between the two fault lines. Earthquakes as powerful as 4.0 occurred a few miles from the San Andreas fault.

How long God will continue to give warning judgment is unknown. The awesome destruction of Oklahoma City on May 3, 1999 (see chapter two), and then the carnage of North Carolina in September 1999 (also chapter two), are strong indicators the warning-judgments are ending. America could be entering into a new level of judgment. This new level could be the dreaded release of the wrath of God on a now reprobate nation.

The governor of California wants his state to be a model for the rest of the nation in the promotion of homosexual marriages. It is very possible that God may make California an example for the rest of the nation of what happens when His wrath falls upon a state which mocks the husband and wife family unit which He created.

> So God created man in his own image, in the image of God created he him; male and female created he them. And God blessed them, and God said unto them, Be fruitful, and multiply, and replenish the earth. . . .
> —Genesis 1:27–28

> Therefore shall a man leave his father and his mother, and shall cleave unto his wife: and they shall be one flesh.
> —Genesis 2:24

March 2000

On March 28, 2000, a powerful tornado ripped through downtown Fort Worth, Texas. The twister actually went right through the downtown area, causing extensive damage to high-rise buildings. This tornado received national attention.

On March 28, 2000, the United States Supreme Court heard a Texas case involving school prayer. In the past, the court has blocked prayers involving public schools. On the radio news, the two news items were back to back. The unprecedented tornado in a major Texas city and the Supreme Court hearing a Texas case involving school prayer! *USA Today* had the two articles touching each other in the March 29, 2000, edition of the paper. The headlines of the articles read, "Tornado rips through downtown Fort Worth" and "Pre-game prayers go to high court, Powerful groups line up on either side of a case in Texas town." The very day that the Supreme Court heard the Texas case to stop school prayer, one of Texas' major cities was devastated by a tornado.

April 2000

On April 4, 2000, the United States House of Representatives debated the issue of banning a hideous method of killing babies called partial-birth abortion. This was the third time the House had debated this legislation. Twice before the House had passed legislation to ban this method of killing babies, and twice the president had vetoed it. The House passed by enough votes to override the veto, but the Senate failed to overturn the veto. On April 5, the House again passed the partial-birth abortion ban.

On April 4, the stock market went into a tailspin. The combined loss on the Dow and Nasdaq were 1,000 points. The market was in convulsions as the House was debating this legislation! At the end of the day, the market recovered. The newspapers had articles titled "Wild Ride on Wall Street" and "Markets' Wildest Ride." The market was in total chaos the very day the House was debating the legislation for banning partial-birth abortions. Could the failure to ban the partial-birth abortion method of killing children be the issue that causes the awesome wrath of God to fall on America?

February 2001

The city of Seattle held a Mardi Gras event to coincide with the famous one in New Orleans. This event always involves drunkenness and sexual immorality. The event in Seattle degenerated into several days of rioting, vandalism, and brutal assaults, along with the drunkenness and sexual immorality. Early in the morning of February 28, the police arrested the last of the rioters, which ended the Mardi Gras celebration in Seattle.

A few hours later, the city and region was rocked by a

powerful 6.8 earthquake. The quake literally hit as the Mardi Gras ended! This earthquake caused over $1 billion in damage, but there was very little loss of life. The quake severely damaged the state capitol building in Olympia. This was the worst earthquake in the Seattle area in 40 years and it occurred at the very end of a week of debauchery, drunkenness, rioting, and violence. The earthquake and the violence at the Mardi Gras were both reported on the same page on the March 1, 2001, issue of *USA Today*. The earthquake article was titled "Seattle glad wallop wasn't worse," and the violence was reported in "Mardi Gras brings injuries, arrests."

It seems the sin of Seattle has reached the attention of God and a clear warning has been sent. This very well maybe the last warning sent to this city.

Summary

This is not an exhaustive study of the correlation between abortion/homosexuality and natural disasters that have hit America. I am limited in time and research tools, but from the research that has been done, clearly God has begun to confront the open and bold sin of America. It is extremely noteworthy that research of disasters, prior to the 1987 homosexual march on Washington, has not lead to any correlation between a specific abortion/homosexual event and a natural disaster. Prior to 1987 these disasters were not that frequent.

The October 1987 homosexual march on Washington seems to have been the event which has triggered these warning-judgments on America. Since this event, the correlation is unmistakable. Could the homosexual march of 1987 be the event which signals that God will no longer tolerate the open and bold sin of America?

When God warns a nation in such a manner as He has been doing with America, it means the nation's sin is at a crisis level with Him. All the warning lights, bells, alarms, and signals should now be on full alert. Have we as a people lost the complete fear of God? Are we so hardened in sin that we cannot see the clear judgment hand of God on the nation: "The wicked shall be turned into hell, **and all the nations that forget God**" (Ps. 9:17). Are we so swollen in pride that we cannot imagine that God would be offended with the death of at least 1.5 million of His children a year, and with homosexuals marching boldly (sometimes naked) down the streets of America's largest cities: "Pride goeth **before destruction**, and an haughty spirit before a fall" (Prov. 16:18).

In examining God's warning-judgments, it appears, if America continues on this collision course with God, America can expect an economic meltdown that might reduce the nation to a third world status. It is crystal clear that powerful earthquakes, the type which level cities and devastate entire regions of the country, can be expected. Powerful hurricanes and tornadoes will destroy entire cities. The Bible so clearly states, "The land is defiled: therefore I do visit the iniquity thereof upon it, and the land itself vomiteth out her inhabitants" (Lev. 18:25). The earthquakes hurricanes, tornadoes, and floods that have recently struck America, along with the economic upheavals, are only warnings.

Listed below is a condensed view of the economic, hurricane, flood, and earthquake warning-judgments that have recently fallen on America.

Economic
1. On October 11, 1987, the homosexuals marched on Washington. During the week immediately following this march, the stock market fell 235 points, and on October 19, it fell over 500 points for a total of 735 points. For the percentage of stock market loss, this was the great-

est crash in history. The 500-point drop up to this date was the greatest one-day drop in history.

2. On October 11, 1989, there were several pro-abortion victories. On October 13, 1989, the stock market plunged 190 points in one hour. Up to this date, this was the second greatest one-day plunge in history.

3. Gay Pride Week and the Gay Olympics took place between June 18 and 26, 1994. During this exact time, the dollar plunged to record lows, and the stock market plunged almost 200 points.

4. On March 8, 1996, a jury acquitted Dr. Kevorkian, which followed a federal court decision to allow physicians assisted suicides. The stock market plunged 171 points, for the third greatest one-day plunge in history up to this date.

5. On July 12, 1996, the House of Representatives debated the Defense of Marriage Act. In counting the days before and after the debate, the stock market plunged 259 points. On July 15, 1996, the next business day after the debate (the debate was on a Friday), the stock market plunged 161 points, for the fourth greatest one-day plunge in history up to this date.

6. On October 8, 1997, Congress passed the ban on partial-birth abortion. On October 10, the president vetoed this ban. On October 6, the stock market went into a steep decline until October 27 when it fell 554 points in one day. This was the single greatest one-day fall to this date.

7. On July 17, 1998, the stock market reached an all-time high until that date of 9,337. On July 23, the market fell 195 points and continued to decline until August 31 when it fell 513 points. During this time period, the market lost 20 percent of its value. On July 23, 1998, the United States House Representatives for the second time passed a partial-birth abortion ban.

8. On April 4 and 5, 2000, the House again debated and

voted to pass legislation to ban partial-birth abortions. While the House was debating this legislation, the market fell 1,000 points and then recovered toward the end of the day.

9. There were several major downturns in the stock market that coincided with forcing Israel to give away the covenant land. These downturns are documented in chapter two.

On January 14, 2000, the stock market had reached an all-time high of over 11,722 points. After the crash of 1987, the market recovered and went on a steady climb toward 11,000. Every sharp downturn occurred during some event in which God's Word warns of judgment. After the event was over, the market would resume its upward climb. It seems the downturns were like road blocks to get the nation's attention. The stock market downturns all coinciding with these events gives a powerful picture of what the future holds for the economy.

Which abortion or homosexual event will push God past the point of no return? How many aborted babies will God tolerate before He moves in judgment? Americans have made an idol out of money and the stock market. God is clear that He is going to smash this idol. God has given warning after warning about the coming judgment on the economy. America has been warned.

The Hurricane Connection
Since Hurricane Hugo, nearly all the hurricanes that have hit the United States since 1989 have been related to national sinful events. Hurricanes Hugo, Bob, Erin, Opal, Bertha, Fran, and Danny all hit the United States in direct connection to a failed pro-life position by the president; pro-abortion legislation by the Congress; a pro-abortion decision by the Supreme Court; the House of Representatives and Senate debating the Defense of Marriage Act; and

a national event to save babies from being aborted.

Hurricanes Andrew, Emily, Dennis, Irene, and Floyd also hit the U.S. in connection with God's judgment. These hurricanes did not hit on abortion or homosexual related events. They will be covered in the next chapter.

Could all this be just a coincidence? Or is it judgment from God? Considering all the other disasters that have occurred during abortion and homosexual related events, these could not have been a coincidence. These hurricanes are an awesome example of how the shedding of the blood of innocent children in the womb and open homosexuality has brought the wrath of God on the nation. America has been warned.

The 500-Year Floods and Then Droughts

Between June 1993 and January 1995, five major floods struck different areas of the United States. The areas hit by the severe rain and flooding were the Midwest, western Georgia, eastern Texas, southern Florida, and California. Four of the floods were categorized by the scientists as being caused by rains so severe that they occur once every 500 years. Thus the rains and ensuing floods were very rare.

During the 18-month period between June 1993 and January 1995, there were four 500-year floods. It is just incredible that four 500-year floods should hit the United States in such a short period of time. These floods were located in the Midwest, western Georgia, east Texas, and California.

After 1995, the 100- and 500-year floods continued all over the nation. The floods hit Ohio, Kentucky, North Dakota, California, and Florida. The 100- and 500-year floods were hitting with such frequency that the news media hardly mentioned this. In addition to the floods, the worst ice storm of the century hit New England in 1998 causing awesome damage.

Starting in 1996, droughts began to spread over America. Texas and the West have repeatedly been subjected to droughts. By 2000, nearly all of Texas came under a drought emergency. The summer of 1999 witnessed the most severe droughts since records were kept for New England and the Northeast. During the summer of 2000, the prolonged drought in the West contributed to the worst forest fires in the nation's history. By the end of August, the fires had burnt 7 million acres.

The frequency of the 500-year storms and droughts has radically increased in the 1990s. The damage done by these storms and droughts has been enormous. God has warned America.

Seismologists and Sin

Between April 1992 and October 1999, southern California experienced four of some of the most powerful earthquakes to occur last century. The earthquakes were all within a very close distance to each other. The earthquakes were: *Joshua Tree*, 6.1, April 23, 1992; *Landers*, 7.6, June 28, 1992; *Big Bear*, 6.5, June 28, 1992; and *Hector Mine*, 7.1, October 16, 1999. Three of the earthquakes fell directly on the day of a national sinful event, while the Hector Mine quake occurred just a few days later.

Because of the potential devastation caused by earthquakes, seismologists and geologists intensely study them. All of these earthquakes were the subject of intense study. This research developed some astounding information which could have dire consequences for California.

The scientists studying these quakes believe that they are all connected as the first earthquake, Joshua Tree, directly lead to the others. These earthquakes occurred in a domino effect. This is amazing because of the timing. A series of powerful earthquakes were tied directly to a series of national sinful events. The pressure of one earthquake led to the next. It is like the spiritual and physical realms are somehow tied together.

The great danger of these earthquakes is the effect on the San Andreas fault. This is the fault which, if ruptured, would devastate California, resulting in multitudes of dead and injured and incredible property damage. Let's look at what the scientists have found about these earthquakes and how the increasing boldness of national sin may culminate in the destruction of California.

The earthquake sequence begins on April 23, 1992, and the United States Supreme Court hearing the *Planned Parenthood v. Casey* case. This case had tremendous national implications as it was thought it could be used by the court to overturn the *Roe v. Wade* case of 1973. On this very day the Joshua Tree quake occurred.

The Joshua Tree quake was alarming to seismologists. This quake tore a 15-mile gash in the earth and was felt from San Diego to Las Vegas to Phoenix. It caused over 6,000 aftershocks. This quake was very close in proximity to the San Andreas fault line. This earthquake caused a San Andreas Hazard B warning to be declared. This warning meant there was a five to twenty-five percent chance of an earthquake occurring on the San Andreas fault within three days. The quake on the San Andreas did not happen, but the powerful Landers quake occurred two months later. The pressure the Joshua Tree earthquake was believed by the scientists to have triggered the Landers quake.

The last Sunday in June is always Gay Pride Day. In 1992 it fell on June 28. The next day, June 29, the Supreme Court issued the ruling for the *Planned Parenthood v. Casey* case. The court failed to use the Casey case to overturn *Roe v. Wade*. The court upheld that abortion was legal. June 28 was a huge homosexual event and June 29 was a huge pro-abortion victory.

In the early morning hours just before the Gay Pride

Day parade in Los Angeles, the Landers and Big Bear quakes struck. Landers was one of the most powerful earthquakes in the twentieth century. It was the second most powerful since the San Francisco quake of 1906. The Landers quake tore a 53-mile long gash in the earth! The power was so great that it was felt 800 miles away and set off earthquakes all over the western part of the nation. The Big Bear quake occurred three hours later and was reported by scientists to be directly connected to the Landers quake. The faults of the two earthquakes were very close, only 20 miles apart.

The scientists found the southern part of the Landers quake fault was moved during the Joshua Tree earthquake and these two earthquakes were connected. The Landers quake then triggered the Big Bear quake just three hours later. Scientists became alarmed by the pressure the Joshua Tree, Landers, and Big Bear earthquakes were putting on the San Andreas fault. These three earthquakes plus the San Andreas fault made a triangle! The Joshua Tree and Landers quake faults were on a line northwest from the San Andreas fault. The Landers fault touched the Big Bear fault. Big Bear then went south back toward the San Andreas fault. Thus, the faults formed a triangle. The scientists are extremely concerned about these earthquakes and the stress they put on the San Andreas fault. The EQE International (engineers who analyze earthquakes for risk management) expressed this concern in an article titled "The Landers and Big Bear Earthquakes." Their concerns follow:

> Scientists are currently studying the possibility that these earthquakes may be related to a future event on the San Andreas Fault, which, together with the geological structures discussed above [Joshua Tree and Landers faults], form a triangle of faults. According to the USGS

[United States Geological Survey], there is a 60 percent chance within the next 30 years that a M8 earthquake will strike the San Andreas Fault somewhere between the Salton Sea and Palmdale.

Given that the USGS estimates a 60 percent chance within the next 30 years of a M8 earthquake striking along the San Andreas Fault, these two quakes and the M6.1 event of April **should be taken as a major warning.** Many seismologists are concerned that these events could be **the beginning of a sequence of events that will lead to the expected major San Andreas event in this region**

According to the scientists, these earthquakes could be the beginning of the sequence to rupture the San Andreas fault. It is very possible that the Joshua Tree quake on the very day of the Supreme Court's abortion case, may be the very day the scientist will pinpoint as the beginning of the sequence that triggered the San Andreas fault.

For seven years this area was free of major earthquake activity. Then, on October 2, 1999, the governor of California signed pro-homosexual legislation. On October 10, the legislation was filed, and on October 14 the governor made a speech stating that California was going to be a model for homosexual rights for the rest of the country.

On October 16, 1999, the powerful 7.1 Hector Mine earthquake struck only 15 miles from the location of the Landers quake seven years earlier. Like the previous quakes in this sequence, the Hector Mine quake was in the desert and did little damage; however, its power was felt from Los Angeles to Phoenix. It generated over 11,000 aftershocks. Like the Landers quake, this one also triggered earthquakes far from its own zone. The Landers quake triggered earthquakes exclusively north of the epicenter, while this one triggered quakes southward as far as the Mexican border.

What troubled the scientists was that Hector Mine triggered a series of quakes very near the San Andreas fault 130 miles away. They referred to this as the faults "talking" with each other. After two weeks, the quakes had stopped near the San Andreas fault.

The scientists believe that the area where these earthquakes are occurring have been inactive for several thousand years. The sudden occurrence of four major quakes in seven years are indications they are all related. One earthquake is setting the stage for the next. Instead of the massive Landers quake decreasing pressure, it actually increased the pressure that helped trigger the Hector Mine quake. In the May 10, 2001, issue of *Nature*, Dr. Andrew M. Freed states the following:

> Stress changes in the crust due to an earthquake can hasten the failure of neighboring faults and induce earthquake sequences in some cases. The Hector Mine earthquake in southern California M7.1 occurred only 20 km from, and 7 years after, the 1992 Landers earthquake M7.3. This suggests that the Hector Mine earthquake was triggered in some fashion by the earlier event.

Dr. Freed then went on to state that all these earthquakes— Joshua Tree, Landers, Big Bear, and Hector Mine—are in a sequence. Freed stated:

> The June 1992 Landers earthquake M7.3, was part of an earthquake sequence that began with the April 1992 M.6.1 Joshua Tree preshock and continued with the M6.2 Big Bear aftershock only a few hours after the Landers rupture.

The scientists are showing a strong correlation in the sequence of these earthquakes. They are trying to identify the triggering device. These earthquakes are dangerously close to the massive San Andreas fault, and the Hector Mine quake actually triggered small earthquakes near this fault. This sequence of quakes is following precisely a sequence of national sinful events. It seems the physical and spiritual realm are running on parallel tracks that are touching each other. Could the sinful acts be the triggering device the scientists are looking for? Could April 23, 1992, be the date that started the countdown sequence toward the massive San Andreas earthquake which will devastate California? The breaking of God's moral laws are clearly effecting the physical laws.

On October 2, 1999, Governor Davis signed into law several bills which advanced the homosexual agenda. One such bill was A.B.537 which went into effect January 2000. This bill created the California Student Safety and Violence Prevention Act of 2000. This act calls for the teaching of tolerance for the acceptance of "alternative lifestyles" to all students K–12. It is very possible that this type of legislation could lead to more massive earthquake activity, heading to the San Andreas rupture. God is not hiding the judgment; He is telegraphing it. These earthquakes are all pointing to the San Andreas fault. In fact, they have all formed a triangle!

It seems the judgment has been set and the rebellion against God will bring it on. God has allowed the quakes on days of national sinful events. There is no reason to believe that the earthquake sequence has ceased, as the boldness to promote homosexuality, even to our children, is accelerating. There was a seven-year gap between the Landers and Hector Mine quakes. The continuing boldness to promote homosexuality and abortion means the pressure for the next massive earthquake is building and building. It is no coincidence these powerful earthquakes are falling directly on days of national sin. The warnings from God are crystal clear, without any doubt. Scientists estimate that there is a massive quake along the southern San Andreas fault approximately every 150 years. The last time was January 9, 1857. It is very possible that the next massive quake could be the tearing of the dreaded San Andreas fault.

Earthquakes

The full impact of God's warning-judgments on America can be seen when you realize that since October 1989, eight major earthquakes have hit California, and one in Washington. These earthquakes have all been in conjunction with abortion or homosexual related events: "He looketh on the earth, and it trembleth: he toucheth the hills, and they smoke" (Ps. 104:32). The nine follow:

1. June 28, 1992—*Landers quake**—Gay Pride Day, followed by Supreme Court decision not to overturn *Roe v. Wade* (third greatest earthquake in the twentieth century to hit mainland USA.)
2. October, 17, 1989—*Loma Prieta quake*—Two days after huge pro-abortion march in San Francisco (tied as fifth greatest earthquake in the twentieth century).
3. October 16, 1999—*Hector Mine quake*—Two days after California governor declared he wanted the state to lead America in homosexual domestic partnerships, and two weeks after the this legislation was passed (tied as sixth greatest last century).
4. April 25, 1992—*Petrolia quake*—Height of attack against the national Operation Rescue event in Buffalo, New York (tied as sixth greatest earthquake last century).
5. January 17, 1994—*Northridge quake*—Day after Sanctity of Life Sunday and five days before the twenty-first anniversary of Roe v. Wade.

---

* This earthquake was the most powerful in the world in 1992. Ten of the most severe earthquakes in the world in 1992 were located in California.

6. June 28, 1992—*Big Bear quake*—Gay Pride Day and Supreme Court decision not to overturn *Roe v. Wade*.

7. April 23, 1992—*Joshua Tree quake*—Supreme Court abortion case hearing and attack against Operation Rescue in Buffalo, New York.

8. September 12, 1994—Next to last day of Cairo conference. The U.S. through Vice President Al Gore tried to push for universal abortion rights throughout world.

9. February 28, 2001—*Seattle, Washington, quake*—Seattle held a Mardi Gras event to coincide with the one in New Orleans, rioting, fighting, etc. ensued during this event. Literally, at the very end of the Mardi Gras the earthquake occurred.

> Defile not ye yourselves in any of these things: for in all these the nations are defiled which I cast out before you: and the land is defiled: therefore I do visit the iniquity thereof upon it, **and the land vomiteth out her inhabitants**.
>
> —Leviticus 18: 24–25.

Chapter Two

The Israel Connection

Hardly a day goes by without some news about Israel and Jerusalem. Israel has become the focus of world attention. Israel has been the subject of several United Nations resolutions. In 1997 the United Nations voted five times to condemn Israel for building apartments in Jerusalem. Nearly all the countries of the world voted against Israel.

The land of Israel and especially Jerusalem have become the focus of world attention. The peace plan in the Middle East involves Israel giving disputed land to the Palestinians for peace. This plan was initiated in 1991 by President George Bush. The disputed land is called the West Bank, Gaza, and the Golan Heights. This peace plan also involves Israel giving East Jerusalem to the Palestinians as their capital. The ruins of the ancient Jewish Temple are located in East Jerusalem.

The world is so sensitive about Jerusalem that in 1980 when Israel moved its capital from Tel Aviv to Jerusalem, nearly all the nations refused to recognize Jerusalem as the capital. The nations kept their embassies in Tel Aviv! Though the United Nations and America initiated the peace plan, there is tremendous pressure on Israel over the land.

Even though the nations of the world are politically against Israel, this country is totally unique. Israel is the only country in the world in which the land was a promise by God. The nation of Israel is based on the faithfulness of God's promise in the Bible. The promise was made 4,000 years ago by God to Abraham, the father of the Jewish people.

This promise or covenant with Abraham was everlasting. God promised to Abraham and his seed (descendants) the land we now know as Israel for an everlasting possession. This promise is found in Genesis 17:7–8:

> And I will establish my covenant between me and thee and thy seed after thee in their generations for an everlasting covenant, to be a God unto thee, and to thy seed after thee. And I will give unto thee, and to thy seed after thee, the land wherein thou art a stranger, all the land of Canaan, for an everlasting possession; and I will be their God.

This promise of the land was also confirmed with Abraham's son, Isaac (Gen. 26:2–4), and his grandson, Jacob (Gen. 35:11–12). About 450 years later, God reconfirmed this promise with Abraham's descendant Joshua (Josh. 1:3–4). With this promise of the land of Israel being given to Abraham and his descendants, the Jewish people and the nation of Israel became extremely important in God's dealing with mankind.

God has chosen the Jewish people and the nation of Israel as a vehicle to reveal Himself to mankind. Through the Jewish people came the Bible, because nearly all the scriptures, both New and Old Testaments, were written by Jews. God has linked His name to Israel. The world can witness God's power and the faithfulness of His Word through His dealings with Israel. Perhaps the most important reason for Israel was the Messiah, the Savior of mankind, who was born as a Jew in Israel.

The promise of the land being given to Abraham and his descendants is of the utmost importance because the authority and faithfulness of God's Word is directly linked with the Jew and the nation of Israel. The promise to Abraham must be fulfilled or the Word of God would be void. The Jewish people and the nation of Israel are tangible proof to the authority and the divine origin of the Bible. You can test the Scriptures by God's dealing with Israel.

At the time of Moses, about 1500 B.C., God made a second promise with Israel. The Law, which reflects God's righteousness and holiness for living in the land, was given to the Jews. The Jews agreed to live by the Law: "And all the people answered together, and said, All that the LORD hath spoken we will do" (Exod. 19:8).

This second promise was conditional. If the Jews obeyed the Law, the promise of God was that they would be greatly blessed; however, if they disobeyed they would be punished, and one punishment would be to be driven from the land and scattered into all the world:

> And the LORD shall scatter thee among all people, from the one end of the earth even unto the other . . . and among these nations shalt thou find no ease, neither shall the sole of thy foot have rest.
>
> —Deuteronomy 28:64–65.

In A.D. 70, the Roman army fulfilled the punishment part of the second promise. The army overran Israel, captured Jerusalem, destroyed the Temple, and scattered the Jewish people into all the world. Remember the Jews were scattered into all the world because they failed to keep the second promise. The everlasting promise with Abraham still stands.

The relationship between the two promises is extremely important, and the following illustration helps to clarify this relationship: Suppose God had made an everlasting promise with the Pilgrims and gave America to them and their descendants forever. In the 1780s God then gave the American Constitution as His standard for living in the nation, and all the people agreed to keep it.

The Constitution was given to show how to live as a "divine citizen" fit for God's presence. God's Name and Word were directly linked with the American people. If they disobeyed and did not live according to His word and holy Name, He promised to drive them from the land into all the world. However, because of the everlasting promise with the Pilgrims, He would never totally destroy the American people. He would one day bring them back into the land. This also would be a sign of His power and righteousness, and the everlasting promise would be fulfilled.

This example is exactly what the Bible says about Israel. Because of disobedience, the Jews would be driven from the land, but never as a people totally destroyed:

> Thus saith the LORD; If heaven above can be measured, and the foundations of the earth searched out beneath, I will also cast off all the seed of Israel for all that they have done, saith the LORD.
>
> —Jeremiah 31:37

The eternal promise with Abraham and his descendants still stands and, based on this promise, the Jews would one day return to Israel from a worldwide dispersion. The nation of Israel would be restored:

> For I will take you from among the heathen, and gather you out of all countries, and will bring you into your own land. . . . And ye shall dwell in the land that I gave to your fathers; and ye shall be my people, and I will be your God.
>
> —Ezekiel 36:24,28

The nation of Israel is extremely important in God's dealing with man. The nation can be viewed as a timepiece for God's redemptive plan for man. Jesus Christ Himself said that Israel can be viewed as a timepiece:

> And they shall fall by the edge of the sword, and shall be led away captive into all nations: and Jerusalem shall be trodden down of the Gentiles, until the times of the Gentiles be fulfilled.
>
> —Luke 21:24

The Gentiles are the non-Jewish peoples.

In May 1948 Israel was reborn as a nation, after being destroyed in A.D. 70. Israel was reborn as the prophets in the Bible had predicted. In June 1967, the Jews were once again in full control of Jerusalem. Jesus Christ said that Israel and Jerusalem would be destroyed until a specific time was fulfilled. With the nation of Israel restored and Jerusalem under Jewish control, God's prophetic calendar is now moving forward.

There are additional prophecies in the Bible which are awesome regarding the Jews and the nation of Israel. God's Word says that those that bless Abraham and his descendants will be blessed, and those that curse them will be cursed: "And I will bless them that bless thee, and curse him that curseth thee: and in thee shall all families of the earth be blessed" (Gen. 12:3). God says the Jewish people are the apple (pupil) of His eye and those that touch Israel touch the apple of His eye: "For he that toucheth you toucheth the apple of his eye" (Zech. 2:8). God says that when the nations come against Israel, He becomes furious and will move to defend His people called by His name:

> And it shall come to pass at the same time when Gog shall come against the land of Israel, saith the Lord God,

that my fury shall come up in my face. For in my jealousy
and in the fire of my wrath have I spoken.

—Ezekiel 38:18–19

There have been many empires through the centuries that
have tried to destroy the Jews, the latest being Nazi Germany. In the end, the Nazis and Germany were destroyed.
In May 1945, the Nazis surrendered, and three short years
later, in May 1948, Israel was reborn as a nation. The atroci-
ties the Nazis committed against the Jews led directly to
the rebirth of Israel! It is a direct challenge of God's Word
to try and destroy the Jewish people or drive them from
Israel. The Nazis tried, and it resulted in their destruction
and the rebirth of Israel!

The prophet Joel said that God will judge the nations
that have touched the Jewish people and parted the land of
the nation of Israel:

For, behold, in those days, and in that time, when I shall
bring again the captivity of Judah and Jerusalem, I will
also gather all nations, and will bring them down into
the valley of Jehoshaphat, and will plead [punish, judge]
with them there for my people and for my heritage Israel,
whom they have scattered among the nations, and parted
[divided] my land.

—Joel 3: 1–2

The prophet Zechariah said that God will defend Israel and
Jerusalem. God will destroy the nations that come against
Jerusalem, even though all the nations of the earth be gathered against it. Jerusalem will be the center of world attention and military action:

Behold, I will make Jerusalem a cup of trembling unto
all the people round about, when they shall be in the

siege both against Judah and against Jerusalem. and in
that day will I make Jerusalem a burdensome stone for
all people: all that burden themselves with it shall be cut
in pieces, though all the people of the earth be gathered
together against it.

—Zechariah 12:2–3

And it shall come to pass in that day, that I will seek to
destroy all the nations that come against Jerusalem.

—Zechariah 12:9

In 1991 President George Bush forced Israel into a peace
process with the Palestinians and Syrians. The heart of the
peace process was for Israel to give land for peace. The
land to be given away was part of the land grant God had
given Abraham. Seven years after the peace process started,
the center of the land to be given away became Jerusalem.
The United States became the prime force in this peace
process of pressuring Israel give away its land. The Bible
says God will judge the nations which have parted the land
of Israel. The city of Jerusalem will become a burdensome
stone, and the nations will be cut in pieces as they come
against it.

The United States has come against Jerusalem and has
challenged God's Word. In November 1991, President Bush
started the peace process and President Clinton continued
it. President Clinton has pressured Israel to give away large
sections of the land, and he has said Jerusalem is negotiable. He has condemned Israel for building apartments
in East Jerusalem. Presidents Bush and Clinton have
brought America into a confrontation with God over the
land of Israel and Jerusalem.

Since November 1991 God has warned America that
the nation is on a collision course with Him over Jerusalem. As America has pressured Israel to give away land,

warning-judgments have hit. Like the abortion- and homosexual–related warnings, these warnings have fallen on the
exact day of pressuring Israel. In fact, some of the warnings regarding Israel have coincided with abortion and
homosexual events. America now has a threefold confrontation with God—abortion, homosexuality, and Jerusalem.

The following are examples of the warning-judgments
which have occurred as the United States has pressured
Israel to give away land and interfered with Jerusalem.

November 1991

After the Gulf War ended in 1991, President Bush began
the initiative to start a Middle East peace plan involving
Israel, the Palestinians, and the countries surrounding Israel. The talks were scheduled to begin on October 30, 1991,
in Madrid, Spain. On October 30, 1991, President Bush
opened the talks with a speech.

On October 31, in their opening speeches, both the Syr-
ian and Palestinian delegations said that for peace Israel
must give away land. At the very beginning of these talks,
the land of Israel was the key issue. The saying by Syria
and the Palestinians was land for peace.

On October 30, a powerful storm developed off Nova
Scotia. The storm was never classified as a hurricane because its sustained winds reached only 73 m.p.h. To be classified as a hurricane, the sustained winds must be 74 m.p.h.
This storm was extremely rare, because it traveled for 1,000
miles in an eastward to westward direction. The weather
pattern for the United States is westward to eastward. The
storm was called extratropical because it didn't originate
in the tropics, as most hurricanes do.

On October 31, this ferocious storm smashed into New
England. The storm was described as a monster, as it was
hundreds of miles wide. This storm was later called "The
Perfect Storm," and a book was written and a movie made

about this storm. The book and movie were called *The Perfect Storm*. This storm was described by meteorologists as one of the most powerful storms to have ever occurred! Extremely rare weather patterns that happen once every 100 years came together to create this monster storm. The ocean waves were over 100 feet high, which were the highest ever recorded. The Perfect Storm ran down the East Coast into the Carolinas, doing millions of dollars in damage. The storm damaged the entire East Coast from Maine to Florida. Remember, this storm was going the wrong way! The damage caused by this storm was classified with that of powerful hurricanes.

The Perfect Storm even heavily damaged President Bush's home in Kennebunkport, Maine. Eyewitnesses said that waves as high as 30 feet smashed into the president's seafront home. The president had to cancel speaking engagements to go and inspect the damage done to his home.

As President Bush was speaking in Madrid, an extremely rare and powerful storm developed in the North Atlantic Ocean. The storm then struck the entire East Coast from Maine to Florida as the Madrid Peace Conference was taking place. The storm even heavily damaged the president's personal home!

The front-page headlines of *USA Today* on November 1 even had the Madrid conference and the Perfect Storm next to each other! One article was titled, "One-on-one peace talks next." The article touching was titled, "East Coast hit hard by rare storm."

At the very beginning of the peace plan involving Israel, a rare and powerful storm smashes into the entire East Coast of the United States. The Perfect Storm heavily damaged President Bush's home, who was the initiator of the Madrid peace plan. The connection between dividing the land of Israel and judgment on the nation causing it was tied together on the front page of America's largest national newspaper. On October 31, 1991, America was put on notice by the Lord God of Israel.

August 1992

On August 23, 1992, the Madrid Peace Conference moved to Washington, D.C., and the talks resumed. The nations involved felt the United States was a better location to continue the talks. The key issue remained that Israel had to give away land for peace.

On August 23, 1992, Hurricane Andrew smashed into southern Florida. Hurricane Andrew was the worst natural disaster ever to hit America. It left 180,000 in Florida homeless, and another 25,000 in Louisiana. The damage was estimated as high as $30 billion. This was an awesome category-four hurricane, with top winds recorded at 175 m.p.h.; however the wind measuring device was destroyed before the eye hit. The winds may have been as high as 200 m.p.h.! This storm was described by the National Hurricane Center as a 25 to 30 mile wide tornado!

Hurricane Andrew hit the day the peace conference met in Washington, D.C. One of the greatest natural disasters ever in American history hit the very day of the conference for Israel to give away its land took place. This conference was originated by President Bush and was now moved to America soil.

On August 24, the front-page headlines of USA Today were: "1 Million flee Andrew," "This will make Hugo look weak," and "Monster storm targets Fla." Also on the front page was an article titled "Mideast peace talks to resume on positive note." America again was hit with a powerful natural disaster in direct connection with the Madrid peace plan.

The connection between dividing the land of Israel and judgment was right on the front page of the nation's largest national newspaper. God is not hiding anything.

September 1993

On September 1, 1993, the front-page headline of the *New York Times* newspaper was: "Israel and PLO Ready to Declare Joint Recognition." The subtitle was: "Meet Secretly in Europe." The article went on to say that diplomatic action was going on secretly in Europe. The agreement reached was that Israel would give away Gaza and Jericho to the Palestinians, followed quickly by the rest of the West Bank. The agreement was to be signed in Washington. The issue of Jerusalem was not addressed in this accord, but it was put off for two years.

Also on the front page as a headline was an article titled "Hurricane Hits Outer Banks as Thousands Seek Safety Inland." Hurricane Emily had meandered across the Atlantic Ocean for five days, but finally hit North Carolina the very day of the peace accord agreement! This hurricane had 115 m.p.h. winds. It brushed the coast of North Carolina, and it then turned and headed out to sea. The damage caused by this hurricane was light.

This was the third hurricane to hit the United States on the very day of a key event of the peace process for Israel to give away land. The headline articles about the hurricane and Israel were actually touching each other! This is another clear warning from God broadcast on the front page of a national newspaper that the nation is on a collision course with Him over the land of Israel!

January 1994

On January 16, 1994, President Clinton met with Syria's President Hafez Assad in Geneva. They met to discuss peace between Israel and Syria. President Clinton said that Syria was ready for a peace agreement with Israel that will include Israel giving the Golan Heights to Syria. (The Golan is the border between Syria and Israel. Israel gained this territory in 1967 during war with Syria. This is part of the land God gave to Abraham.) The newspapers quoted President Clinton as saying, "Israel must make concessions that will be politically unpopular with many Israelis."

Less than 24 hours later, a powerful 6.9 earthquake rocked southern California. This earthquake was centered in Northridge, about 25 miles from Los Angeles. The quake was the second most destructive natural disaster to hit the United States. It was second to Hurricane Andrew. This earthquake was literally under the feet of the center of the pornography industry of America! It also occurred only a few hours after Sanctity of Life Sunday and a few days before the anniversary of *Roe v. Wade!* The quake also destroyed several abortion centers.

Less than 24 hours after President Clinton was pressuring Israel to give away land, America was rocked by a powerful and damaging earthquake. This occurred only hours after Sanctity of Life Sunday! What an awesome warning-judgment to America. This earthquake hit in direct connection to abortion, pornography, and forcing Israel to part the land! Some of the greatest natural disasters to hit America—Hurricane Andrew and the Northridge earthquake—occurred exactly on the days America was pressuring Israel to give away its land.

God warns in the Bible that He will judge nations as they deal with Israel. It is crystal clear that America has come under the judgment hand of God for its dealing with the nation of Israel!

March–April 1997

On March 1, Yasser Arafat left Israel and arrived in Washington, D.C., to meet with President Clinton. They met to discuss a Jewish housing project being built in East Jerusalem. This is the section of Jerusalem which is claimed by the Palestinians. The Israeli government had begun to build 6,500 housing units in East Jerusalem in an area called

Har Homa. Arafat was upset and met with President Clinton to discuss this issue.

Arafat was given a warm welcome by President Clinton. The *New York Times* reported the meeting with an article titled "Welcoming Arafat, Clinton Rebukes Israel." The president rebuked Israel for building the housing in Jerusalem, and he condemned Israel for creating mistrust.

Arafat went on a speaking tour of the United States and was warmly received. He spoke in the United Nations about the situation in Jerusalem. In one speech, he used the example of the Vatican in Rome as an example of what should happen in Jerusalem—a Palestinian city within Jerusalem.

The issue of Israel building homes in Jerusalem upset the entire world. On five separate occasions between March 6 and July 15, the United Nations Security Council and the General Assembly voted to condemn Israel for building homes in East Jerusalem. The entire world was upset because Jews were building houses Jerusalem! A percentage of these homes were to be for Arabs.

On March 6, the Security Council voted to strongly criticize Israel. The resolution said that the housing was a violation of international law and a threat to peace in the Middle East. The United States vetoed the resolution which prevented it from becoming official. Outside of the U.N., the Clinton Administration condemned Israel for the building project. The issue was then taken to the General Assembly.

On March 13, the General Assembly voted to condemn Israel over building homes in East Jerusalem. The vote was 130–2 to condemn Israel. Only Israel and the United States voted against the resolution. Fifty-one nations failed to vote. The resolution said that the housing was illegal and a major obstacle to peace. This vote showed the strength of feeling as to how unified the world was against Jerusalem. The Clinton Administration continued to condemn Israel outside of the U.N. All this international condemnation of Israel was over building homes in Jerusalem!

On March 21, the Security Council again voted to condemn Israel and once again the United States vetoed the resolution. The U.S. criticized Israel outside the U.N. for the housing project. On April 25, the General Assembly demanded by a 134–3 vote that Israel stop the housing project in Jerusalem. The resolution also called for international action against Israel. The U.S. voted against the resolution.

On July 15, the General Assembly again voted by 131–3 for a resolution to condemn Israel for the housing project. This was the strongest resolution yet, as it called for an economic boycott of products made in Jewish settlements in the disputed areas of Israel including Jerusalem. The U.S. voted against this resolution.

From March 1, when Arafat traveled to America, until mid-April, Israel was constantly under criticism by the Clinton Administration for the housing project in Jerusalem. The U.S. supported Israel in the United Nations, but outside of the U.N., Israel was constantly criticized by President Clinton.

On the very day Arafat landed in America, powerful tornadoes devastated huge sections of the nation. (For more detailed information on these storms, please see chapter one, heading March 1997.) While Arafat was on a speaking tour, which was against Israel, these storms stalled over Ohio and caused tremendous flooding. The tornadoes destroyed Arkadelphia, Arkansas, while the flooding destroyed Falmouth, Kentucky. The storms did over $1 billion in damage. Also, heavy snows fell in March and April in the Northern Plains. These snows melted and in April caused the worst flooding in a century in the Dakotas. This was also a billion-dollar disaster.

While Arafat toured America, some of the worst tornadoes hit along with awesome floods. Remember that God will judge the nations that divide the nation of Israel. Arafat was using America as a platform to promote the dividing of Israel. He was warmly received by President Clinton! The president's own home state was devastated by the tornadoes!

The connection between President Clinton meeting with Arafat and condemning Israel, and the destructive tornadoes that devastated Arkansas was captured by the *New York Times*. On March 4, 1997, the front-page headlines said, "In Storms Wake Grief and Shock." Directly touching this article was a picture of President Clinton with Arafat, and the heading of the picture said, "President Clinton Rebukes Israel." The front page of a national newspaper actually had the destruction of the tornadoes and rebuking of Israel touching each other! The *New York Times* put it together so clearly!

In addition to Arafat's visit, President Clinton signed legislation on March 1 to release millions of dollars overseas which could be used for abortion. On March 3, Congress began its second debate on banning the partial-birth abortion procedure. This debate lasted through most of March, and on March 21 the House voted a second time to ban partial-birth abortions. The abortion issue and dividing the land of Israel coincided during most of March 1997.

On March 11, the stock market reached an all-time high of 7,085 points. The market had been steadily increasing since October 1996. On March 13, the U.N. General Assembly voted overwhelmingly to condemn Israel, and on this day the stock market plunged 160 points. The market continued to plunge until April 13, when it stabilized and then continued its upward climb. Between March 13 and April 13, the market lost 694 points.

On April 7, President Clinton met with Israeli prime minister Benjamin Netanyahu to discuss the peace process and the building of homes in Jerusalem. This meeting coin cided with the plunge in the market. Prime Minister Netanyahu refused to stop the building of the homes in Jerusalem. After this meeting, the attacks against Israel over the land of Jerusalem subsided. President Clinton stopped the condemnation of Israel. Very soon after this, the stock market stabilized.

From March 13, when the General Assembly first condemned Israel, until after the meeting with Netanyahu, the stock market dropped 694 points. The drop in the market and the crisis over Jerusalem was again front-page stories in a national newspaper. On April 3, the *New York Times* front-page article was titled "The Mideast Muddle." A small article touching it was titled "Stock Downturn Resumes."

March and April 1997 were awesome months for God dealing with America. The combination of Arafat coming to America; Clinton rebuking Israel over not giving away land; and abortion activity coincided with some of the worst tornadoes and flooding this century. It also coincided with the storms in the Dakotas which resulted in the worst flooding ever. These disasters resulted in damages of over a billion dollars. Entire towns were destroyed, like Arkadelphia, Arkansas; Falmouth, Kentucky; and Grand Forks, North Dakota. The Bible states that God will judge the nations that divide the land of Israel. In March and April the land of America suffered terribly as pressure was put on Israel.

As the U.N. condemned Israel over Jerusalem, the stock market began to melt down. The very day of the General Assembly's condemnation of Israel over Jerusalem, the market began a month-long slide. The U.S. stock market affects the entire world. As the world through the U.N. came against Israel, the world's largest stock market was shaken. It is interesting to note that both Wall Street, the location of the market, and the U.N. are both located in New York City. The land of America and the stock market were judged at the same time over Jerusalem.

July 1997

On July 2, Thailand devalued its currency. The world's leading economic nations paid no attention to this devaluation. However, this act by Thailand began to destabilize the entire world economy. By devaluing its currency, Thailand could handle its debt better. It made Thailand's exports cheaper; thus the nation was more competitive on the world market.

Soon after Thailand devalued its currency, nearly all the nations of Asia did the same. One by one the nations currencies fell, and then their stock markets began to fall. Thailand, South Korea, Philippines, Indonesia, Hong Kong, Japan, and other nations stock markets began to collapse. By October, the panic spread to America, and on October 27 the stock market fell 554 points. The stock market did recover and continued to climb toward 10,000.

The world's economy was shaken by this. There were headlines in the newspapers such as "Market dive circles globe." The devaluation of Thailand's currency in July turned into a world economic crisis only three months later. This crisis affected the world economy and drastic measures were undertaken to prop up these Asian countries. The failure of Japan would shake the entire world economy.

In March and April 1997, the United Nations voted four times to condemn Israel for building homes in Jerusalem. On July 15, 1997, the U.N. General Assembly again voted by 131-3 to condemn Israel for building homes in Jerusalem. This was the strongest resolution against Israel. The resolution called for identifying all products produced in the disputed areas and then boycotting these products. The U.N. had economically come against Israel. While the U.N. was drafting plans against Israel, Thailand devalued its currency on July 2, which started the shaking of the entire world's economy. A very short time later, the entire world economy was in turmoil.

The entire world through the United Nations came against Israel in March and April 1997. On July 15, 1997, the world tried, through a boycott, to punish Israel economically. On July 2, the world economy started to unravel. Jerusalem and the land of Israel had taken center stage in world politics. The United Nations wants the disputed land in Israel given away and Jerusalem divided. As the nations were planning to economically punish Israel, the world economy was shaken. Many nations in Asia were reduced to poverty. The economic meltdown, which started in Asia, then spread to Russia, and later Brazil. None of these nations voted to support Israel in the United Nations. As the nations of the world are coming against Israel, they are being destroyed.

> And in that day will I make Jerusalem a burdensome stone for all people: all that burden themselves with it shall be cut in pieces, though all the people of the earth be gathered together against it.
>
> —Zechariah 12:3

Jerusalem has become a burdensome stone for the nations, and they are being cut in pieces as they come against *the apple of God's eye.*

January 1998

On January 21, Israeli prime minister Netanyahu met with President Clinton. The meeting was to discuss the stalled peace plan and for Israel to give away some of its land. In the lead-up to the meeting, Netanyahu was under tremendous political pressure. Clinton was pressuring Israel to give away the land for the peace process. In Israel there was pressure on Netanyahu not to give away land. The pressure was so great that politicians in Israel threatened to pull down his government if he gave away the land.

Netanyahu met with Clinton and was coldly received. Clinton and Secretary of State Albright refused to have lunch with him. Shortly after the meeting ended, a sex scandal involving Clinton became headline news. Clinton became totally involved in the scandal. Clinton couldn't devote any time to Israel. He met with Arafat the next day, but there was no effort to pressure Israel to give away land.

Netanyahu came to the meeting with the possibility that his government might fall. How ironic that literally right after the meeting, it was President Clinton's administration that was in trouble. The president was humiliated and faced legal action. The very day Clinton was pressuring Israel to give away land, he was humiliated in a sex scandal. Netanyahu returned to Israel as a "conquering hero" because he did not give away any land.

Because of this scandal, the legal action against the president continued until he appeared before a grand jury on August 17. After his grand jury appearance, the president addressed the nation and admitted he had misled the grand jury when he testified under oath in January. On September 9 the report of the investigation of the president was sent to the House of Representatives for possible impeachment and removal from office. On October 8, 1998, the House of Representatives voted for an impeachment inquiry of President Clinton. On December 19, 1998, the House of Representatives passed two articles of impeachment against President Clinton, and sent the articles to the Senate for a trial.

The sex scandal involving Clinton broke almost five years to the day that he issued five executive orders reversing years of abortion limitations. On the day after his inauguration in 1993 and on the eve of *Roe v. Wade*, he issued these orders. (For details of the abortion activity on this day, see chapter one, heading January 1998.)

Exactly five years later, almost to the very day, this sex

scandal involving the president was international headline news. The sex scandal that rocked the presidency coincided with the anniversary of his abortion executive orders and forcing Israel to give away land!

September 1998
On September 24, 1998, President Clinton announced he was going to meet with Yasser Arafat and Israel's prime minister, Benjamin Netanyahu, when they both came to New York City to address the United Nations. The purpose of the meeting was to discuss the stalled peace plan in which Israel was to give away an additional 13 percent of its land. On this same day, the headlines of the national newspapers said that Hurricane Georges was gaining strength and heading toward the Gulf of Mexico. The headlines of *USA Today* stated, "Georges gaining strength, Killer storm zeros in on Key West."

On September 27, Secretary of State Madeleine Albright met with Arafat in New York City in preparation for the meeting with the president. Albright was working out final arrangements for Israel to give away 13 percent of its land. On September 27, Hurricane Georges slammed into the Gulf Coast with 110 m.p.h. winds, with gusts up to 175. The eye of the storm struck Mississippi and did extensive damage eastward into the Florida panhandle. This hurricane hit the coast and then stalled. The hurricane moved very slowly inland and dumped tremendous amounts of rain which caused tremendous flooding.

On September 28, President Clinton met with both Arafat and Netanyahu in the White House. The meeting was to finalize Israel giving the land away. The three agreed to meet on October 15 to formally announce the agreement. The headlines of *USA Today* stated, "Georges lingers." The article next to it was, "Meeting puts Mideast talks back in motion." The newspapers actually had the hurricane and

Israel peace talks next to each other on the front page! The *New York Times* also had the hurricane and peace talks together on the front page.

On September 28, Arafat addressed the United Nations and talked about an independent Palestinian state by May 1999. Arafat was given a rousing and sustained ovation as he addressed the General Assembly. As Arafat was speaking, Hurricane Georges was smashing the Gulf Coast, causing $1 billion in damage! Arafat finished and then left America. Hurricane Georges then dissipated.

At the exact time Arafat was in the United States for the purpose of carving up Israel, Hurricane Georges was pounding the Gulf Coast. Arafat left America and the hurricane then dissipated! God judges the nations that divide His land.

October 1998

On October 15, 1998, Yasser Arafat and Benjamin Netanyahu met at Wye Plantation, Maryland, to continue the talks which ended on September 28. The talks where scheduled to last five days and were centered around Israel giving away 13 percent of the West Bank land. The talks stalled and President Clinton pressured them to continue until a settlement was reached. The talks were extended and concluded on October 23. In the end, Israel agreed to give away the land for assurances of peace by Arafat.

On October 17, awesome rains and tornadoes hit eastern Texas. The San Antonio area was deluged by 20 inches of rain in one day! The rains caused flash floods and destroyed thousands of homes. Rivers swelled to incredible size. The Guadalupe River, which was normally 150 feet wide, swelled three to five miles wide. The floods were so powerful that entire small towns were nearly swallowed. The rains and floods continued until October 22 (the end of the Middle East talks) and then subsided. The rains and floods ravaged 25 percent of Texas and did over $1 billion in damage.

On October 21, President Clinton declared this section of Texas a major disaster area, and directed the Federal Emergency Management Agency (FEMA) to assist in the relief for the flood-ravaged families. This was a record flood that hit Texas.

For almost the entire time of the Middle East talks, awesome rains and storms were smashing Texas. The national newspapers once again had the Middle East talks and disaster together on the front page! As the talks ended, the storms and flooding in Texas ended. Once again President Clinton had to declare a section of America a disaster area at the exact time he was meeting with Arafat to carve up Israel!

November 1998
The stock market recovered from the crash of July–September and went on to record levels. The week of November 23 the market reached its all time high. On November 30, Yasser Arafat came to Washington, D.C., and met with President Clinton. Arafat came to raise money for his Palestinian state, and he also said that in May 1999 he was going to declare a Palestinian state with Jerusalem as the capital.

A total of 42 other nations were represented at this meeting in Washington. All the nations together agreed to give Arafat $3 billion in aid. President Clinton promised that the United States would give $400 million and the European nations pledged $1.7 billion.

As President Clinton was meeting with Arafat, the stock market was crashing, and it fell for a total of 216 points this day. The economic pundits could not explain why the stock market crashed other than for profit taking. The radio news reports for November 30 had the Mideast meeting and the stock market crash as stories following each other. The meeting and the crash were headline stories the next day in some of the nation's newspapers. The articles were even touching each other on the front page.

On December 1, the European stock markets crashed for the third worst crash in European history. How ironic that as the nations of the world met to promise $3 billion dollars in aid for a Palestinian state, their own stock markets crashed! This happened literally to the day for the United States and the very next day for Europe.

As the nations of the world continue to come against God's covenant land of Israel and Jerusalem, their economies fall under judgment. America is now leading the world into a direct confrontation with God over Jerusalem. God's Word clearly says He will destroy the nations that come against Jerusalem!

December 1998

On Friday, December 11, 1998, the Judiciary Committee of the House of Representatives began to deliberate articles of impeachment against President Clinton. On December 12, the committee completed the deliberation and voted to approve four articles of impeachment against the president. The committee then forwarded the articles to the House for a vote on impeachment.

What is truly amazing is that as the committee was voting on the four articles of impeachment, President Clinton was landing in the Palestinian-controlled section of Israel! He agreed in October to come to Israel to insure the Wye Agreement moved forward, and the timing was such that it occurred at the exact time articles of impeachment were drawn against him! Literally as he was landing in Israel the four article of impeachment was being drawn against him! On December 11, the headline articles of major newspapers had the impeachment and Clinton going to Israel on the front page. The radio and television news stories had the stories back-to-back. The Associated Press reported that the president went to Israel, **"Under an impeachment cloud."** The articles of impeachment and Clinton's Mideast trip were tied together by every type of media. No one following news could miss that the articles of impeachment against Clinton were completed while he was in Israel forcing the Jews to give away the covenant land!

The news sources reported that the president was the first in U.S. history to visit Palestinian-ruled territory, and that his visit was giving statehood status to the Palestinians. The capital of this state is to be Jerusalem! These same news sources reported that Clinton was the first president in 130 years to be impeached!

On December 15, President Clinton returned to Washington. Just four days later the House of Representatives voted to accept two of the articles of impeachment against the president. The articles were then sent to the Senate for a trial and upon conviction the president would be removed from office.

I watched the political pundits who were astonished that the House voted for impeachment. The various pundits said that up to two weeks before the impeachment it was clear the House did not have the votes to impeach. The pundits said that in the last two weeks, many congressmen became enraged with the president over this. Just before the president left for Israel, he made a public speech about the impeachment which further enraged congressmen. I thought back, and two weeks before the impeachment vote was when Arafat came to Washington and Clinton promised to give him $300–500 million in support. The president had 42 other countries agree to raise a total of $3 billion for Arafat. At this exact time, the hearts of many congressmen were turning against the president and for impeachment!

God's Word is crystal clear that all who come against God's covenant land and especially Jerusalem will be destroyed. At every turn of the impeachment against the president has been his forcing the Jewish people to give away the covenant land.

March 1999

On March 23, Yasser Arafat met with President Clinton in Washington, D.C., to discuss a Palestinian state with Jerusalem as its capital. On March 24, Arafat went to the United Nations to discuss Palestinian statehood. On March 23, the stock market took the biggest fall in months. The market fell 219 points while Arafat was meeting with Clinton to carve up the nation of Israel.

On March 24, President Clinton authorized the attack on Serbia. The top military leaders in Russia made statements that World War III had begun. Vikto Chechevatov, a three-star general and commander of ground forces in Russia's Far East region, said this attack "was the beginning of World War III." Russia called for the draft of 200,000 soldiers. Russia mobilized its fleet and sent them into war maneuvers. During the maneuvers, Russia actually sent its bombers on a mock attack mission against America. The bombers were intercepted near Iceland and turned away from the route to America. Russia began to redeploy its tactical nuclear weapons. Russia had threatened NATO and America that the bombing of Serbia could lead to direct conflict with Russia.

The backdrop of the attack of Serbia was massive homosexual political activity across the entire 50 states (see March 1999 heading of chapter one) and Arafat meeting with Clinton to carve up Israel. On June 9, 1999, Serbia withdrew it forces from Kosovo and the tension over Serbia subsided.

The long-term effect of this attack on Serbia was hostile relations developed between America and both Russia and China. Russia and China entered into a military alliance. Russia supplied China with some of its best naval vessels and attack aircraft. China became very aggressive in its threats against America. The attack on Serbia has changed the entire course of world diplomacy. It is the opinion of this author that the attack on Serbia in the long run will be seen as the event which changed the long term stability of the world. Only time will tell if this event will lead to a confrontation between the nations.

May 1999

On May 3, 1999, starting at 4:47 p.m. (Central Standard Time), the most powerful tornado storms to ever hit the United States fell on Oklahoma and Kansas. The wind of one tornado was officially measured at 316 m.p.h., making it the fastest wind ever recorded. This tornado was very near to being classified as an F-6 on the tornado rating scale. There has never been an F-6 tornado. The storm included many F-4 and F-5 tornadoes (F-5 have winds over 260 m.p.h.) which are extremely rare. There were almost 50 confirmed tornadoes with nearly 200 warnings! One F-5 tornado was over a mile wide and traveled for four hours, covering 80 miles on the ground. It destroyed everything in its path. This tornado was unprecedented in the history of tornadoes. F-5 tornadoes make up less than one percent of all tornadoes. Tornadoes are usually a couple of hundred yards wide at the most, not over a mile; they seldom last for more than 10 to 15 minutes, not four hours; they stay on the ground for a couple minutes, not four hours.

The damage of this storm was incredible. The headlines of the newspapers stated: "Everything was gone—At least 43 dead in monstrous Plains tornadoes"; "20 hours of terror"; "Stark scene: Miles of devastation"; "Tornadoes shred state." The National Oceanic and Atmospheric Ad-

ministration stated, "This is an outbreak of historic proportions, no doubt about it." Oklahoma governor Frank
Keating said, "This is the most calamitous storm we've ever
seen and probably one of the more calamitous that ever hit
the interior of the United States."

In Oklahoma City alone, more than 2,000 homes were
destroyed. Entire small communities disappeared as everything in the towns were leveled. The town of Mulhall, Oklahoma, ceased to exist. Thousands of automobiles and ve-
hicles were destroyed. The total for the damage is in the
billions of dollars. On May 4, parts of the states of Oklahoma and Kansas were declared federal disasters areas.

The storm warnings began at 4:47 p.m. (CST). In Israel this would have been 1:00 a.m. on May 4. May 4 is the
date Yasser Arafat was scheduled to declare a Palestinian
state with Jerusalem as its capital. This declaration was
postponed until December 1999 at the request of President
Clinton. President Clinton has already stated that the Palestinians should have their own state, that Jerusalem was
negotiable, and he even refused to move the United States
embassy to Jerusalem. On May 4, President Clinton declared
parts of Oklahoma and Kansas disaster areas. On this very
same day, the president sent a letter to Arafat. In the letter,
Clinton encouraged Arafat's aspirations for his "own land,"
said the Palestinians had a right to "determine their own
future on their own land," and that the Palestinians deserved
"to live free, today, tomorrow and forever."

What an awesome warning to America. The most powerful tornadoes to **ever** hit the United States fell the same
day (May 4, Israeli time) that Arafat was to proclaim a Palestinian state with Jerusalem as its capital. The United
States has forced Israel into this "peace process" and pressured Israel to already give away some of the covenant land.
President Clinton has been the major force supporting Arafat. The very same day Clinton encouraged Arafat about

the Palestinian state he declared parts of America a disaster area from the worst tornadoes in history.

It appears the rebellion of the American people against God is very soon coming to a climax. If America continues to pressure Israel to give away the covenant land and encourage Arafat, these type disasters and even greater can be expected. The disasters could be on a magnitude **never** before seen in our nation. The declaration of a Palestinian state with Jerusalem as its capital, backed by the government of the United States, could release the dreaded wrath of the holy God of Israel on our nation.

September 1999

In late August, Hurricane Dennis began to affect the East Coast. This hurricane moved very slowly up the coast, drenching the states of Florida, Georgia, South and North Carolina. This was not a powerful hurricane, being listed as a Category 2 with sustained winds of 105 m.p.h. Although this hurricane was not powerful, it had tremendous rainfall.

Hurricane Dennis slowly moved up the coast and then stopped directly east of the Outer Banks of North Carolina. Dennis began to act very strangely. After stalling off North Carolina, it actually started backward along the course it came. Then the hurricane reversed itself and came back along the same course. It then stalled again off the Outer Banks and began to drift eastward. Finally, on September 3, after five straight days of lingering off the coast, Dennis struck North Carolina. Dennis' winds diminished quickly and did not cause tremendous damage. Dennis dropped tremendous amounts of rain, and flooding occurred.

On September 1, Secretary of State Madeleine Albright flew to the Middle East. Albright met with several Arab leaders before meeting with Yassar Arafat and Israeli prime minister Ehud Barak on September 3. The purpose of

Albright's visit was to restart the Wye Agreement which had stalled. This agreement, reached in October 1998, involved Israel giving away land for peace. As a result of this meeting between Albright, Arafat, and Barak, the talks were restarted and both sides agreed to have the final agreement for Israel to give land for peace by September 12, 2000. Both sides agreed to meet on September 13, 1999, to begin the final talks, which would be concluded by September 2000.

Hurricane Dennis lingered off the coast of North Carolina nearly a week. The hurricane traveled in a bizarre path. At one point it actually reversed itself, and at another time was **heading away** from the coast. At nearly the exact time Albright met in Israel, using the power of the United States to assist in Israel giving away the covenant land, Hurricane Dennis came ashore! This hurricane was literally doing circles in the Atlantic Ocean until the meeting in Israel. On this very day, the hurricane then hit the United States. Remember, this hurricane did not do tremendous damage, but it did drop enormous amounts of rain. This would prove to be extremely important just two weeks later when Hurricane Floyd hit.

On September 13, 1999, the Israeli foreign minister and one of Arafat's deputies met to work out arrangements for what is called the "Final Status" of Israeli giving land away. This meeting was a result of Albright's trip the week before. They agreed that by February 15, 2000, to present outlines for the borders of the Palestinian state, the status of Jerusalem, and the Jewish settlements in the West Bank and Gaza Strip.

On September 13, 1999, Hurricane Floyd strengthened into a very dangerous Category 5 storm, with sustained winds of 155 m.p.h. The forecasters at the National Hurricane Center were astonished how quickly Floyd grew in size and strength in one day. The actual statement was,

"Floyd grew unexpectedly into a monster of a storm on Sunday." This was the very day the meeting was taking place in Israel to give away the land.

On September 16, Hurricane Floyd slammed into North Carolina. Floyd's winds had diminished to 105 m.p.h., which was a Category 2, but this hurricane was huge in size. Hurricane-force winds extended 150 miles in front of it. This hurricane caused the greatest evacuation in the history of the United States. As the storm moved up the coast, literally millions of people were evacuated in front of it. The awesome destructive force of this storm was the rains. Rains of 20 inches or more fell over the entire eastern part of North Carolina. The rivers were still swollen and the land soaked from Hurricane Dennis, which had hit just two weeks before. The destruction of this storm was awesome. The entire eastern section of the state, some 18,000 square miles, was destroyed.

In North Carolina, 28 counties declared a state of emergency. Some 400 to 500 roads were closed. Farmers estimated over 100,000 hogs, 2.47 million chickens, and over 500,000 turkeys were dead. Huge amounts of horses and cattle also died. Sewage and water systems were knocked out. Sewage, chemicals, and dead animals all flowed into the rivers creating an environmental nightmare. Some entire counties were nearly totally destroyed. The damage to agriculture was estimated at $1 billion, but could exceed this amount. The loss to buildings, homes, and roads was in the billions. This was the greatest disaster to hit North Carolina since the Civil War.

While Israel was meeting with Palestinians to give away the covenant land, almost the entire East Coast of America was being ravaged by a monster hurricane. This hurricane grew into a monster the very day of the first meeting to reach the Final Status in the Middle East peace accord. This meeting was set by Secretary of State Albright just one week earlier! The land of Israel is being torn by pressure from the United States, and at the exact time the land of America is being ravaged by awesome destruction!

On September 21, the Dow Jones Industrial Average fell 225 points, for the steepest loss in four months. On September 22, the stock market lost 74 points, and the next day, September 23, the market fell 205 points. The total loss for the three days was 504 points. This was the first time in the history of the stock market it suffered two 200-point losses during the same week! What was amazing about the loss was that it coincided exactly with Arafat visiting President Clinton to discuss the Wye Agreement. They met on September 22, the day between the two 200-point losses on the stock market! Arafat then left Clinton and went to the United Nations. There, he asked the U.N. to back independence for a Palestinian state. The stock market dropped 524 points for the week that Arafat came to discuss the Wye Agreement and visit the U.N.

September witnessed some of the greatest destruction in United States history. This coincided exactly as the plan by President Clinton to have Israel give away the covenant land was being implemented. Arafat came and met with the president, and at that exact time the stock market had record losses.

October 1999
During the week of October 11, Jewish settlers on 15 West Bank hilltops in Israel were evicted. This eviction was resisted by the settlers and the confrontation was reported in the national media during the week. Remember, President Clinton is the power behind Israel giving land for peace. On October 16, the *New York Times* ran a front-page article about this confrontation titled "On the West Bank, a Mellow View of Eviction." What is amazing is that also on the front page was an article titled "Big Sell-Off Caps Dow's

Worst Week Since October '89." During the week, the market lost 5.7 percent, and it was the worst week since October 1989.

While Israel was forcing the settlers off the covenant land, the stock market was melting down. On October 15, the market lost 266 points! Also on October 15, Hurricane Irene hit North Carolina, and on the morning of October 16, a powerful 7.1 earthquake rocked the Southwest.

On October 16, the fifth most powerful earthquake to hit America in the twentieth century struck California. The earthquake was 7.1 in magnitude and was located in the desert in a sparsely populated area. The earthquake did little damage, but shook three states. The earthquake was so powerful that it tore a 25-mile gash in the earth. Millions of people in California, Nevada, and Arizona felt the power of the quake. This quake triggered small quakes near the San Andreas fault, which was 120 miles away. Seismologists referred to this as a "nerve-rattling conversation" between the two fault lines. Earthquakes as powerful as 4.0 occurred a few miles from the San Andreas fault.

In a 12-hour span, the stock market closed down 266 points, a hurricane hit the East Coast, and the West Coast was rocked by a huge earthquake. This all occurred as Jewish settlers were being evicted from the covenant land!

January 2000

On January 3, 2000, President Clinton met with Ehud Barak, Israeli prime minister, and Farouk al-Shara, the foreign minister of Syria. They met to discuss peace between Israel and Syria. This peace plan is for Israel to give back the Golan Heights. The Golan Heights is critical to the defense of Israel. When Syria controlled the Golan Heights, it was used as a position for the artillery to fire into Israel. The talks were to last two days, January 3 and 4, 2000. On January 4, Israel's prime minister agreed to hand over five percent of its territory to the Palestinians, and the transfer was to be completed by the end of the week. The hand-over of this land came from previous agreements brokered by President Clinton.

By December 31, 1999, the stock market had reached its all-time high. On January 4, 2000, the stock market plummeted. Both the Dow and Nasdaq plunged. The Dow fell 359 points for the fourth worst one-day decline, and the Nasdaq fell 229 points for the worst drop ever. The combined losses in money for the one day was $600 billion. For the days of the meetings to pressure Israel to give away the covenant land, the stock market was reeling with losses. When the meetings were completed, the market recovered the losses and it went on to register huge gains. The *New York Times* reflected on the stock market activity for the week with an article titled "The 3 U.S. Stock Gauges Rally to End a Turbulent Week." The turbulent week on Wall Street occurred exactly as the meeting was taking place to have Israel give away the Golan Heights and Israel agreed to give away five percent more of the West Bank.

April 2000

President Clinton summoned Israel's prime minister, Ehud Barak, to Washington, D.C., for a conference regarding the peace process. They meet on April 12. During the meeting, Clinton requested that he wanted to get more involved with the peace process. This process involves Israel giving away the covenant land and possibly the dividing of Jerusalem. Barak agreed to Clinton's request.

On April 11–13, the Nasdaq section of the stock market collapsed. For these three days, the market fell over 600 points. The Nasdaq is the section of the stock market where the high-tech stocks are traded. During the 1990s, the Nasdaq has grown to $4 trillion dollars in value. The Nasdaq has an enormous impact on the economy. For the week, the Nasdaq fell 618 points for the worst week ever.

At the precise time that Israel's prime minister was in Washington to meet with Clinton, the stock market was collapsing into the Nasdaq's worst week in its history. There is an apparent connection between Barak and Arafat coming to America to discuss the peace process and huge convulsions in the stock market. Could the stock market totally collapse someday, at the precise time Israel is being forced to divide the land or Jerusalem?

June 2000
On June 16, 2000, President Clinton met with Yasser Arafat in the White House. They met to discuss the negotiations with Israel which had stalled. President Clinton made the statement, "I want to finish the job," referring to the peace process between Israel and the Palestinians. While in Washington, Arafat said that a Palestinian state would be declared on September 13, 2000.

On this date the stock market fell 265 points. The market collapsed in the final hour of trading and was the lowest closing in months.

July–August 2000
Starting on July 12, 2000, President Clinton, Israeli prime minister Ehud Barak, and Palestinian leader Yasser Arafat met at Camp David, Maryland, to try and reach an agreement for peace. The talks continued until July 26, when they collapsed. The talks collapsed over Jerusalem. President Clinton personally was involved in trying to divide Jerusalem into Moslem and Jewish sections. The talks also involved giving away huge sections of land to Palestinian control, which the president supported. No agreement was reached. Statements were made by Arafat that a Palestinian state was going to be declared with or without an agreement. Tension became very high after the meeting.

As the meeting was talking place, tremendous forest

fires began to erupt in the West. The fires exploded in intensity at the end of July and then burned out of control during August. By the end of August, the fires had burnt nearly 7 million acres and were reported as some of the worst of the century. The states of Montana and Wyoming were declared disaster areas. There was no hope of putting the fires out, and only the winter snows and rains could do it. All forest fire fighters in America were fighting these fires. The army and national guard was called to help fight the fires. Fire fighters came from all over the world to help. More than 25,000 people were battling the fires.

The weather conditions for the fires were reported as the equivalent for the Perfect Storm. Agriculture Secretary Dan Glickman reported that weather patterns over the western section of America were ideal for the fires, and were similar to conditions that created the Perfect Storm. There were high temperatures, low humidity, lightning storms with no rain, and high winds. This pattern lasted for months on end.

During the month of July, the rains stopped in Texas. On July 28, Governor George W. Bush declared the state a disaster area for 195 counties because of the drought and fires. The state also went through the entire month of August without rain. The drought of over 60 days was compared to the one which caused the Dust Bowl of 1934. The drought of July–August 2000 was the worst in the state's history.

While the meetings were taking place on American soil to partition Jerusalem and the covenant land of Israel, record-breaking droughts and forest fires were taking place. Entire states were declared disaster areas.

September—December 2000

On September 28, 2000, which was Rosh Hashana, the Jewish New Year, Ariel Sharon, the famous Israeli general went

to the Temple Mount in Jerusalem. The visit sparked rioting. The rioting continued unabated into the summer of
2001. The riots resulted in dozens of Jews being killed and
hundreds of Palestinians. The rioting was attributed to the
failed Camp David meetings in July 2000. During these
meeting, President Clinton had pressured Israel to give
away large areas of Jewish settlements and sections of East
Jerusalem. The sections of Jerusalem included the Temple
Mount. The failure of the Camp David meeting destabilized
the political situation between the Israelis and Palestinians.

By the end of October 2000, Prime Minister Barak's
government had collapsed and Israel was without a government. In the face of the rioting, public support eroded
and the Barak government collapsed. Israel had no government! On December 9, 2000, Barak resigned his position as prime minister and called for new elections. The
elections were set for February 2001. The political situation in Israel immediately stabilized when Barak resigned
and elections were set. From the end of October to December 9, Israel was in political chaos.

The United States held its presidential election on November 7. The election resulted in total political chaos, as
neither candidate was declared a winner. The state of Florida hung in the balance to determine who would be elected.
The election dragged on until the Florida results went to
the U.S. Supreme Court. On December 12, 2000, the court
ruled and George W. Bush was declared the winner. From
November 7 until December 12, the U.S. government was
in chaos. There was no elected government.

The Israeli government was destabilized by the direct
actions of President Clinton. Almost during the exact time
the Israeli government was in chaos, the U.S. government
was destabilized and in chaos. On December 9, when the
election was set in Israel, a few days later the U.S. election
were settled. Both governments were in chaos at nearly

126—God's Final Warning to America

the exact time! What happened to the Israeli government, happened at the same time to the U.S. government. The country that was responsible for destabilizing Israeli was itself destabilized at the very same time!

The U.S. presidential election was in total chaos. The election was held on November 7. President Clinton invited Arafat to Washington to try and renew the peace talks. The peace talks had completely broken down after the Camp David failure in July and the riots which started in September. Arafat arrived in Washington on November 9, as the U.S. was in the worst presidential crisis in over 100 years! Arafat met with President Clinton just two days after the election—while the election process was melting down! On November 9, the media headlines were the political crisis and Arafat meeting with Clinton!

The Results of Arafat's Visits to America

- March 2, 1997: Arafat meets with President Clinton in Washington, D.C. The same day, awesome tornados unleash tremendous damage in Arkansas and floods occur Kentucky and Ohio. Arkansas and Kentucky are declared disaster areas.

- January 21, 1998: President Clinton is waiting to meet with Arafat at the White House. At this exact time, the president's sex scandal breaks.

- September 27, 1998: Arafat is meeting with the president in Washington. Hurricane Georges hits Alabama and stalls. The hurricane stalls until Arafat leaves and then it dissipates. Parts of Alabama are declared a disaster area.

- October 17, 1998: Arafat comes to the Wye Plantation meeting. Incredible rains fall on Texas, which cause record flooding. Parts of Texas are declared a disaster area.

- November 23, 1998: Arafat comes to America. He meets

with President Clinton, who is raising funds for the Palestinian state. That day the stock market falls 216 points.

- March 23, 1999: Arafat meets with Clinton in Washington, D.C. Market falls 219 points that day. The next day Clinton orders attack on Serbia.

- September 3, 1999: Secretary of State Albright meets with Arafat in Israel. Hurricane Dennis comes ashore on this very day after weeks of changing course in the Atlantic Ocean.

- September 22, 1999: Arafat meets with Clinton in Washington, D.C. The day before and after the meeting the market falls more than 200 points each day. This was the first time in history the market lost more than 200 points points for two days in a week. The market lost 524 points this week.

- June 16, 2000: Arafat meets with President Clinton. The market falls 265 points on this day.

- July 12–26, 2000: Arafat at the Camp David meetings. Powerful droughts throughout the country. Forest fires explode in the west into uncontrolled fires. By the end of August, 7 million acres are burnt.

- November 9, 2000: Arafat meets with President Clinton at the White House to try and salvage the peace process. This was just two days after the presidential election. The nation was just entering into an election crisis, the worst in over 100 years.

God has very clearly shown that America is on a collision course with Him over the land of Israel. President Bush was the initiator of the peace plan to give away the land of Israel. On the very day the meeting opened in 1991, a freakish storm originated in the North Atlantic Ocean and heavily damaged the president's home. President Bush's land was damaged. On the day the peace process moved to the United States, the nation's land was devastated by powerful Hurricane Andrew, the worst natural disaster to ever hit America.

President Clinton met with Assad of Syria, and he boldly said Israel had to give away the Golan Heights to Syria. Within 24 hours the land of America was rocked by the powerful Northridge earthquake. President Clinton met with Arafat, and he publicly rebuked Israel. Within 24 hours, Arkansas, the president's home state, was hit by devastating tornadoes. This tornadic storm was one of the worst ever recorded. Arafat then toured America. During the exact time of the tour, some of the worst flooding hit the land of the Ohio Valley. At this same time, powerful snowstorms fell on the land of the North Plains, which eventually helped cause awesome floods.

In March and April 1997, the United Nations condemned Israel over Jerusalem. In July 1997, the U.N. called for a boycott of products coming from the land of Israel. In July 1997, an economic crisis started in Asia that touched the entire world. Billions of dollars were needed to try and stabilize these nations. Nations whose economies seemed to be endlessly growing, overnight were reduced to poverty!

In September 1998, Arafat came to the United States to speak with President Clinton and address the United Nations. Arafat's objective was to force Israel to give away 13 percent of the land and gain recognition of a Palestinian state, with Jerusalem as the capital. The exact time Arafat was in the United States, Hurricane Georges slammed into the Gulf Coast, causing over $1 billion in damage. The correlation between disasters hitting America and forcing Israel over the covenant land continued right into September 2000.

God intends to keep His promise with Abraham and the Jewish people. God will let no nation, including the United States, stand in the way of fulfilling His promise.

America is in an extremely dangerous position before the Lord God of Israel. God has a controversy with the nations over Jerusalem.

> A noise shall come even to the ends of the earth; for the LORD hath a controversy with the nations, he will plead with all flesh; he will give them that are wicked to the sword, saith the LORD.
>
> —Jeremiah 25:31

Israel and Jerusalem are central to God's redemptive plan, because the Bible declares Jerusalem is the location for the second coming of Jesus Christ. Jesus Christ will not return to Washington, London, Paris, Moscow, or Mecca. He will return to Jerusalem.

> Then shall the LORD go forth, and fight against those nations, as when he fought in the day of battle. And his feet shall stand in that day upon the mount of Olives, which is before Jerusalem on the east.
>
> —Zechariah 14:3,4.

> Behold, he that kept Israel shall neither slumber nor sleep.
>
> —Psalm 121:4

Chapter Three

America:

A Nation That Has Rejected God

On June 17, 1963, the United States Supreme Court issued
the final decision in a series that forbids Bible reading and
prayer in the public schools. Bible reading and prayer had
been a part of American schools since the beginning of the
country. The prayer the court objected to follows:

> Almighty God, *we* acknowledge our dependence upon
> Thee, and we beg Thy blessings upon us, our parents,
> our teachers, and our Country.

God had honored prayer by giving America (up to 1963)
the finest educational system in the world. The Scholastic
Aptitude Test (SAT) scores were the highest ever. Prior to
1963 America's violent crime rate fell below the national
population growth rate. The divorce rate was dropping
steadily from the 1940s, and the teenage premarital sex rate
went unchanged. By the 1990s, a separation of church and
state was established and everything to do with God had
been removed from the public schools and many govern-
mental institutions.

　　When the Supreme Court rejected God and His Word,

immediate judgment did not appear to fall. It appeared there were no repercussions and the country continued. At first the judgment for rejecting God was not felt or seen, but 30 years later it is clear that in 1963 the blessings of God were removed from America. Looking back to 1963, it is clear that awesome judgment fell on America.

The year 1963 literally became the year of separation between God's blessings and God's judgment. For the nations that honor God, the Bible states: "Blessed is the nation whose God is the LORD; and the people whom he hath chosen for his own inheritance" (Ps. 33:12). For the nation that rejects God, the Bible states: "The wicked shall be turned into hell, and all the nations that forget God" (Ps. 9:17).

In 1963, the three greatest problems in school were talking, gum chewing, and noise. By the 1990s, the three greatest problems in the godless public schools were rape, robbery, and assault. The SAT scores have literally plummeted since the very year of 1963. America has paid a terrible price for rejecting God. Prior to 1963 serial killings and mass murders were almost unheard of, but today they both occur with frightening regularity, and America is increasingly becoming a more and more violent nation. America's cities have become like those of a third world nation. Sexual diseases have skyrocketed, along with premarital relations in our teenagers.

Since 1963, every statistic showing a social problem has risen dramatically, while the statistics for things that are good have dropped. America is literally being turned into hell, as the Bible predicts would happen to all nations that reject God. More police will not prevent crime. More money will not improve the school system. More taxes will not solve the nation's problems. America needs national repentance for rejecting God and allowing such sins as abortion, adultery, drugs, fornication, homosexuality, and pornography to become common and accepted. The nation needs to turn to Jesus Christ as Lord to be forgiven and healed.

The following charts* document the long-term results on America for rejecting God and His Word. The charts are only a few of many that show that the blessings of God were removed in 1963 as America rejected the living God. America is on a course of total national destruction. How much longer can the country continue on this downward spiral and remain a great nation?

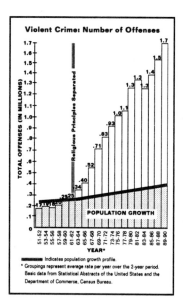

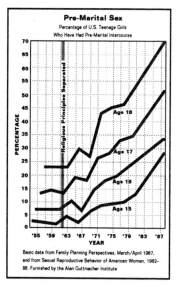

* Charts are from the book titled *America: To Pray or Not to Pray*, by David Barton.

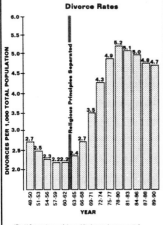

Divorce Rates

"The U.S. is at the top of the world's divorce charts on marital breakups." U.S. News and World Report, June 8, 1987, pp. 68-69.

"The number of divorces tripled each year between 1962 and 1981." Time, July 13, 1987, p. 21.

Basic data from the U.S. National Center for Health Statistics., Vital Statistics of the United States, annual.

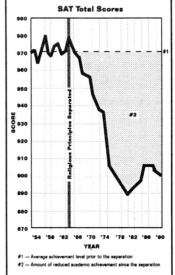

SAT Total Scores

#1 — Average achievement level prior to the separation
#2 — Amount of reduced academic achievement since the separation

Basic data from the College Entrance Exam Board

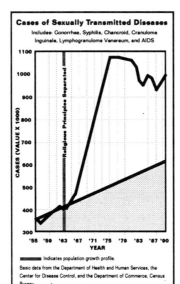

Cases of Sexually Transmitted Diseases

Includes: Gonorrhea, Syphilis, Chancroid, Granuloma Inguinale, Lymphogranuloma Venereum, and AIDS

▬▬▬ Indicates population growth profile.

Basic data from the Department of Health and Human Services, the Center for Disease Control, and the Department of Commerce, Census Bureau.

Chapter Four

America:
The Voice of Thy Blood Crieth
Unto Me from the Ground

On January 22, 1973, the United States Supreme Court overturned all state laws that protected children in the womb and then legalized the killing of children throughout the entire pregnancy. The aborting of babies was actually made a constitutional right by the court! Today, in America, there are "doctors" who actually specialize in killing full-term babies in the womb.

America aborts a reported 1.5 million babies a year, which means, after 20 years, approximately 30 million children have been killed in the womb. Many abortions are not reported, so the real figure is much higher. The figure is so large that it has become meaningless. Abortion is so ingrained in America that politicians, including the president, actually run for office proclaiming their abortion position, and the people still elect them.

Although America has turned its back on defending children in the womb, each child killed was special to God: "Lo, children are a heritage of the Lord, and the fruit of the womb is His reward" (Ps. 127:3). God sends children as a blessing, but Americans literally throw His children, by the millions, in the garbage. God has a plan for the life of each child, and with God there is no such thing as an unwanted child.

God has clearly warned in the Bible that His judgment will fall on any nation that sheds the blood of its children. The killing of babies defiles a country and, "Therefore I do visit the iniquity thereof upon it" (Lev. 18:25). The killing of babies causes God to become furious: "Wherefore I poured my fury upon them for the blood they had shed upon the land" (Ezek. 36:18). God literally hates the shedding of innocent blood: "This does the Lord hate . . . hands that shed innocent blood" (Prov. 6:16–17).

The Bible records the murder of Abel by his brother Cain. The scripture states that the shed blood of innocent Abel cries out to God: "The voice of thy brother's blood crieth unto me from the ground" (Gen. 4:10). With the amount of children that Americans have killed in the womb, the voice of their shed blood must be a deafening roar to God. Their voices cry out for justice.

The Shedding of
Innocent Blood and the Nations

The book of Genesis records a covenant God made with Abraham, who was the father of the Jewish people. In this covenant God promised to bless Abraham and also his descendants by giving them the land now called Israel. God told Abraham that before the Jewish people could possess the land, they would have to leave Caanan (modern Israel) and go to Egypt for 400 years. God said the reason for the 400-year wait to possess the land was that the sin of the people living on it, the Amorites, was not yet at the judgment level: "But in the fourth generation they shall come hither again: for the iniquity of the Amorites is not yet full" (Gen. 15:16). The Bible does not mention what the iniquity of the Amorites was, but for 400 years God worked with these people to stop them from the sin. After 400 years God used Moses to bring the children of Israel back into the Promised Land. The instructions from God were to destroy the inhabitants of the land, the Amorites, because the iniquity was now complete. God then listed the specific sins that brought the judgment. The sins were fornication, adultery, homosexuality, bestiality, and child sacrifice. God told the Jewish people that for these sins the people of the land were being cast out:

> For in all these the nations are defiled which I cast out before you: And the land is defiled: therefore I do visit the iniquity thereof upon it, and the land itself vomiteth out her inhabitants . . . (For all these abominations have the men of the land done, which were before you, and the land is defiled;).
>
> —Leviticus 18:24–25, 27

God went on to warn the Jews that if they practiced such sins, they also would be driven off the land.

The shedding of the innocent blood of children and open sexual sins brought the wrath of God on the Amorites. The sins of the Amorites sound a lot like modern-day America. God in His mercy tried for 400 years to stop the Amorites from sacrificing their children but, in the end, only judgment would stop it. The Amorites were violent people; they killed their children, and God used violence to judge them. They had been inflicting violence upon their own children, and in the end they received the judgment of violence: "I do visit the iniquity thereof upon it" (Lev. 18:25). God used the Jewish people as His instrument of judgment on the Amorites.

The Bible goes on to record the history of the ancient Jewish people. Unfortunately, they also disregarded the

Bible's warning about shedding innocent blood and acted just like the Amorites. God sent prophet after prophet for hundreds of years to try and turn Israel from shedding innocent blood, but Israel became harder and harder against God. Finally, King Manasseh came to power and violence completely overtook Israel. The Bible records that Manasseh sacrificed his own children. He filled Jerusalem with violence: "Moreover Manasseh shed innocent blood very much, till he had filled Jerusalem from one end to another" (2 Kings 21:16). The people of the nation followed Manasseh into violence and killed their children: "Manasseh seduced them to do more evil than did the nations whom the LORD destroyed before the children of Israel" (2 Kings 21:9). This killing of innocent children triggered God's judgment. God used the Babylonians as His instrument of judgment. A huge Babylonian army came and destroyed the nation. The cities were all burned, and hundreds of thousands were killed. The survivors were taken as captives to Babylon for 70 years.

The prophet Ezekiel lived during the time when the Babylonians destroyed ancient Israel. He documented the reason for the destruction. The primary reason was that the Jews had turned from God to paganism, and the heart of paganism was violence and the killing of children. God's wrath fell because innocent blood was continually being shed: "Wherefore I poured my fury upon them for the blood that they had shed upon the land" (Ezek. 36:18). The prophet explained that the killing of children was the specific reason for the judgment:

> And I polluted them in their own gifts, in that they caused to pass through the fire all that openeth the womb, that I might make them desolate, to the end that they might know that I am the LORD.
>
> —Ezekiel 20:26

This verse means that God was bringing judgment because

the Jews sacrificed their firstborn children as burnt offerings to pagan gods.

On January 22, 1973, when killing babies in the womb was legalized, judgment from God did not appear to immediately fall from heaven. There was no apparent reaction from God. Just as after the decision to bar prayer and Bible reading in schools, the country continued on. However, looking back to 1973, it is clear that judgment immediately fell on America. The judgment that began in 1963 for rejecting God was intensified in 1973: "The wicked shall be turned into hell, and all the nations that forget God" (Ps. 9:17). God's blessings that began to be removed in 1963 were fully removed in 1973.

Every year since 1970, Fordham University has produced a study called the Index of Social Health. This index is a study of the quality of life, and it is an overall view of the nation's social health. The index examines all levels of society by measuring 16 key indicators. The levels are: children, youth, adults, aging, and all ages in general. For children, the index examines infant mortality, child abuse, and children in poverty. The key indicators for the youth are teen suicide, drug abuse, and high school dropouts. For adults, the key indicators are unemployment, average weekly earnings, and health insurance coverage. For all ages, the areas examined are homicides, alcohol-related highway deaths, food stamp coverage, access to affordable housing, and the gap between the rich and poor.

This index is unique. It is the only study that combines 16 key indicators into a single measurement to monitor the social well-being of the nation. This index is able to give a long-term view of the direction of the nation. These indicators provide a comprehensive view of the nation's social health. The key indicators are tied directly to the nation's institutions, such as the family and school.

The index combines the 16 indicators into a single rating, with 100 being the highest. The higher the rating, the better the social conditions. The early 1970s ratings averaged around a rating of 73. The highest rating recorded was 76.9 in 1973. The rating started dropping in 1974 and continued to drop until 1991 when it fell to 39.4. This represents a 50 percent decline in less than 20 years! (See chart: Index of Social Health of the United States 1970–1992.)

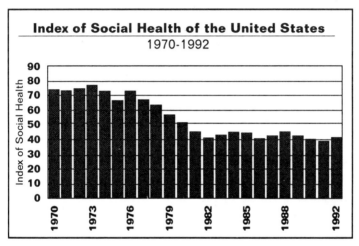

The year after America legalized killing babies in the womb, the terrible social deterioration started! According to this index, 1973 was the high water mark of American society.

Since 1973 society has been crumbling. This deterioration had become catastrophic by the mid-1990s. The current social conditions of America can be traced directly back to 1973 when God's blessings were withdrawn and His wrath fell on the nation. The nation was immediately judged in 1973. It just took some years for the judgment to show.

In November 1993, the Justice Department released the results of a huge survey of the American public. The survey focused on how many Americans were victims of violent crimes since 1973. Many crimes are not reported, so to find the real number of crime victims, 4.4 million people were interviewed. The Justice Department found that 36.6 million Americans were victims of violent crimes between 1973 and 1993. The survey found that the overall crime rate was down, but violent crime has dramatically risen. The sharp increase in violent crime was caused by the youth. America's teenagers and young adults have become extremely violent. This dramatic increase in teenage violence coincides with the legalization of violence against children in the womb.

According to the United States Justice Department, during the summer of 1994 America passed a milestone as the prison population topped one million. This figure does not include local city prison populations, and experts estimate an additional 400,000 are being held in these prisons. The only country with a greater prison population is Russia. The reason for the swelling prison population is the surging violent crime rate.

A very interesting comparison is the crime and abortion rates in Washington, D.C., which is the crime capital of the U.S., with 1,578 per 100,000 of the population in prison. The national average is 373 per 100,000. The abortion rate for Washington in 1992 was 138.4 per 1,000 women, which also makes it the abortion capital. The national average was 25.9 women per 1,000. More babies are aborted in Washington, D.C., than are born. In 1992 there were 21,320 babies aborted in little Washington, D.C. This was more abortions than the combined states of Utah, Montana, Idaho, North and South Dakota, Vermont, New Hampshire, and West Virginia. Given America's current moral state, it is fitting that the nation's capital should also lead the country in the crime and abortion rates.

America is being consumed by violence. The violence against the innocent unborn in the womb has now spread throughout the entire society. Any form of bloodshed always leads to more bloodshed. The Bible refers to this spreading of violence as "bloodshed touching bloodshed."

This spreading of violence can be seen in the number of crimes against young children. According to the National Committee for the Prevention of Child Abuse (NCPCA), there were 607,000 reported cases of child abuse in 1976. By 1993 the number of cases had surged to 2,990,000. Of the 2.99 million cases, 1,017,000 were verified as child abuse. There were hundreds of thousands more cases verified in 1993 than were reported in 1976! The murder of our children is also rising. FBI statistics reveal that in 1973 there were 131 infants murdered in America. By 1990 the number of murders had risen to 264. During 1990 the NCPCA verified that 1,211 children under 14 were murdered, while in that same year a total of 20,045 Americans were murdered. The fastest growing murder rate in America is infants. The violence against children in the womb has clearly spread to all children.

Prior to removing God's Word from the schools and then legalizing abortion, Americans were not violent toward their children. Directly coinciding with the legalization of child killing in the womb has been this surge of violence against all children. The violence against children both in and out of the womb are linked together. It seems that a murdering spirit has been turned loose in America. America's self-restraint against violence has been greatly weakened, and when this happens the Bible states that "bloodshed touches bloodshed."

There are 1.5 million abortions reported every year in America, but not all states have reporting requirements. It is very possible, after 20 years of legalized abortion, that 37 million babies have been killed. This figure is strikingly close to the number of Americans the Justice Department reported were injured by violence since 1973. The current crime rate virtually parallels the abortion rate! It almost seems that for each aborted baby, one American falls victim to a violent crime. The current violence level in America is God's judgment on the nation for the killing of His children in the womb.

The Bible very clearly states that for killing children God will deal with that nation as it deserves: "Therefore I do visit the iniquity thereof upon it" (Lev. 18:25). The violence in the womb is clearly being matched by violence in the streets and cities. America is getting what it deserves! Are the sins of America now like the Amorites—full?

Perhaps the clearest of all judgments is on the economy. The gross national product (GNP) is the sum of all goods and services in a country. A growing GNP is the sign of a prosperous and healthy economy. The chart titled "Real GNP" shows the true GNP of America from 1945 to 1990. Real GNP is when inflation is factored out of the economy. When looking at the chart, notice how the real GNP of the U.S. economy from 1973, except for a few years of upturn,

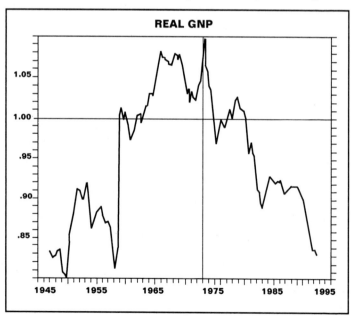

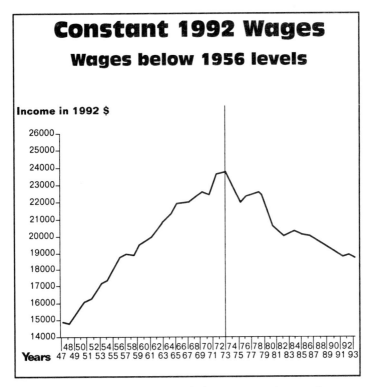

Constant 1992 Wages

Wages below 1956 levels

Income in 1992 $

is in a very sharp decline, and the year 1973 was the very year the American economy began that decline.

The decline in the GNP was followed by a sharp decline in the actual hourly wages of American workers. When the salary of the American worker is adjusted for inflation, the actual salary rate is in a sharp decline. In fact, the chart titled "Constant 1992 Wages" shows that the hourly salary rate peaked in 1972, and since *1973* it has been in decline. The chart covers the time period from 1947 through 1993. From 1947 until 1972 the hourly wage increased every year; however, since *1973* the hourly wage has decreased almost every year. The year 1973 is again pinpointed as the very year that America started its economic decline. The decline is so steep that, if you adjust for inflation, Americans in 1993 earned less, on average, than they did in 1956.

To compensate for this decline and to maintain their standard of living, the American government, businesses, and people went into heavy debt. From 1973 until 1993 the federal government increased spending by 500 percent, while the federal deficit increased from $14.9 billion a year to over $300 billion dollars a year. This was a 2,100 percent increase! The huge debt that America now faces can be traced directly back to *1973* when the economy started its sharp decline. American workers are under a slow but steady punishing economic grind. This is why today both husband and wife have to work to try and keep the same standard of living as one salary did years ago. No matter how hard they work, American workers are falling further behind.

The large salaries of today are an illusion. The foundation of American prosperity is debt and not savings. At some point, this huge debt bubble will collapse. As long as the nation continues to kill its children there will be no blessing from God. The economy will continue to fail until at some point it will collapse.

From 1960 to 1973 the people in poverty in America fell dramatically from 40 million to 22 million. The year with the lowest number of people in poverty was *1973*. After 1973 the poverty rate increased to the point that by 1991 over 34 million Americans were living in poverty. By the end of 1993 the Census Bureau reported the numbers in poverty had reached 39.3 million. This was the same amount of people that were in poverty in 1961. America is going backward—not forward. The year 1973 was literally the dividing line between decreasing poverty and increasing poverty. It is clear that something dramatic happened in 1973.

It is ironic that even the worst bear stock market since World War II began in *1973*. (A bear market is when the market loses rather than increases value over a long period of time. It is a declining market.) The bear market that started in 1973 actually began in January, the same month the United States Supreme Court ruled in *Roe v. Wade* to legalize abortion! Economists identified January 11 as the start of the bear market; *Roe v. Wade* was decided just 11 days later on January 22. The bear market lasted until December 6, 1974, which was a total of 694 days. The Dow Jones Industrial Average went from 1051.70 to 577.60. The market lost 45.1 percent of its value. Until 1998, both the length of days and percentage of loss of this bear market remain the greatest since 1945. (See chart below that lists all the bear markets since 1945.)

BEAR MARKETS

Beginning		Ending		Percentage Change	
Date	**Dow**	**Date**	**Dow**	**Length**	
May 29, 1946	212.50	May 17, 1947	163.21	353 Days	-23.2%
Dec. 13, 1961	734.91	June 26, 1962	535.76	195 Days	-27.1%
Feb. 9, 1966	995.15	Oct. 7, 1966	744.32	240 Days	-25.2%
Dec. 3, 1968	985.21	May 26, 1970	631.16	539 Days	-35.9%
JAN. 11, 1973	**1051.70**	**DEC. 6, 1974**	**677.60**	**694 Days**	**-45.1%**
Sept. 21, 1976	1014.79	Feb. 28, 1978	742.12	525 Days	-26.9%
April 27, 1981	1024.05	Aug. 12, 1982	776.92	472 Days	-24.1%
Aug. 25, 1987	2722.42	Oct. 19, 1987	1738.74	55 Days	-36.1%
July 18, 1990	2999.75	Oct. 11, 1990	2365.10	87 Days	-21.2%

Since 1950, the Department of Labor, Bureau of Labor Statistics, has been charting the American worker's productivity. The statistics show that from 1950 to 1989 the lowest year for productivity was *1973–1974*. It seems the "bottom literally fell out" of the American economy in 1973, and until the mid-1990s it has not recovered.

When all the economic data is correlated, it is quite clear that the American society, and especially the economy, peaked in 1973. The worst recession since 1945 began on January 11, 1973. Because of this recession and the other economic factors that peaked in 1973, it is quite possible that January 1973 can be pinpointed as the very month that the United States economy peaked. The American economy has been on a slow but very steady downhill slope since January 1973. January 1973 virtually can be viewed as the dividing line between a blessed nation and one that has fallen under the judgment of God. It is the opinion of this author that January 22, 1973, the day the United States Supreme Court legalized child killing, was literally the day of economic judgment for the nation. This very day was the "high water mark" of America.

The Homosexual Connection

By the mid-1990s, a large segment of the American population had accepted and/or tolerated homosexuality, but this was not always the case. It was not long ago that all 50 states had criminal laws against homosexuality. What happened that allowed homosexuality to be decriminalized and then to be promoted as being "normal"? Just as abortion was legalized in 1973, so homosexuality was declared to be normal in 1973.

On December 15, 1973, the American Psychiatric Association (APA) issued a position paper declaring that homosexuality was no longer to be classified as a mental disorder. This declaration by the APA altered its almost 100-year position that homosexuality was a mental disorder. It is rather ironic that the Supreme Court decision to legalize abortion also overturned a 100-year law that abortion was a criminal act. The APA in normalizing homosexuality declared that "by itself, homosexuality does not meet the criteria for being a psychiatric disorder." Prior to the change, homosexuality was defined as a sexual deviation, along with fetishism, pedophilia, sadism, voyeurism, and others. The APA went on to state that all criminal laws against homosexuality should be repealed, and civil laws should be enacted at the local, state, and federal level to protect homosexuals.

The APA wanted all areas of American society opened to homosexuals. The position paper declared the laws against homosexuality have "been used as a tool of discrimination in the private sector, and in the civil service, military, Immigration and Naturalization Service, health services, adoption, and child custody courts." This act by the APA literally opened the flood gate for homosexuals.

By the end of the 1990s, only 25 years later, the homosexual agenda as outlined by the APA has reached the point where they are demanding the right to adopt children and have "same-sex marriage" legalized. The explosion of homosexuality into mainstream America can be traced directly back to the APA position paper of December 15, 1973.

The decision by the APA had the effect on homosexuality that *Roe v. Wade* had on abortion. Both decisions radically changed the course of American society, and both decisions were made in 1973. The year began with the Supreme Court legalizing abortion, and it ended with an APA declaration that homosexuality was no longer to be viewed as deviant behavior.

The two issues which bring God's judgment on the nation were declared as legal and normal the very same year— 1973! It is no wonder that 1973 can be pinpointed as the very year that God's blessings were removed from America.

It is interesting to chart the deterioration of America. In 1963 the moral fiber was broken as America turned from God. Statistics show that the divorce rate, crime, etc., began to rise dramatically since 1963. This moral decline was so steep that in just 10 short years abortion was made legal. The moral decline that started in 1963 began to affect the economy, and 1973, the year abortion was legalized, became the very year the economy began to fail. A little over 10 years later, in the mid-1980s, America went from being the greatest creditor to the greatest debtor nation. By the mid-1990s the national federal debt had exploded to $5 trillion. This does not include personal and corporate debt. By 1994, over one million Americans were in prison, and America had become an extremely violent nation. At the present rate of decline, what will the next few years bring?

The year 1973 was a critical year for America. The nation turned its back on the innocent unborn in the womb and legalized abortion. The number of people in poverty stopped its long downward trend and began a long upward trend; the social conditions of America peaked in 1973, and then started a long downward trend; the economy peaked in 1973 and started a long downward trend; 36.6 million Americans were victims of violent crimes between 1973 and 1993, which closely matches the number of aborted babies. America has paid a fearful price for killing innocent children in the womb. What will it take for Americans to realize they are under the judgment of God, and to stop shedding the blood of their children?

> Wherefore I poured my fury upon them for the blood that they had shed upon the land.
>
> —Ezekiel 36:18

Chapter Five

There Is a Way That Seemeth Right Unto a Man, But . . .

To a substantial percentage of the American population, there are two issues about which they will not compromise. The issues are abortion and sexual "freedom," including homosexuality. These two issues seem to be a "sacrament" to these people. Yet, these "sacraments" are the very issues which the Bible clearly states will bring God's wrath on the nation.

The supporters of abortion and gay rights are in positions of great power in the United States. The main media (ABC, *Newsweek*, *USA Today*, etc.) always seems to present these issues in a favorable light. The slogan of the pro-abortion agenda is, "Keep abortion safe and legal." The courts have made abortion a constitutional right, and every year there are more and more court decisions which legitimatize homosexuality. The American Medical Association (AMA) no longer classifies homosexuality as a mental disorder. The AMA and the American Bar Association (ABA) have taken pro-abortion positions.

The atmosphere on most college campuses is openly pro-abortion and pro-homosexuality. Rutgers University in New Jersey has taken the lead in supporting homosexuals on campus. Rutgers has a homosexual dorm with its own assistant dean. The university has a homosexual alumni association, and student fees go to groups that promote homosexual concerns. Many colleges are following Rutgers' example.

The Democratic Party has a taken a pro-abortion position and is pushing for legalizing homosexuality through civil rights-type legislation. Some states, such as Washington, allow homosexuals to adopt children. Some cities, such as San Francisco, and states, such as Massachusetts, recognize homosexual relationships as equivalent to a marriage and give these people all the benefits of a married couple. There have been court decisions in Hawaii that recognize a homosexual marriage as equivalent to a heterosexual marriage.

America is a long way down the road to accepting homosexuality as an "alternate lifestyle," and abortion as an absolute "right" of a woman to do with her body as she pleases. Although most Americans do not favor abortion as birth control or completely accept homosexuality, the power structures of society have been taken over by those that do. There seems to be a moral void, a lack of inner strength, a lack of willingness to stand for God's principles by multitudes of Americans. This has resulted in great advances by those who promote the very issues which remove God's blessings and bring forth His wrath.

Even though the power structure of America, along with multitudes of people, accept abortion and homosexuality as "human rights," the Bible states: "There is a way that seemeth right unto a man, but the end thereof are the ways of death" (Prov. 16:25). The Bible warns us that there are lifestyles which lead to physical death and, in eternity, spiritual death. Spiritual death means separation from God. Abortion and sexual immorality, the two issues which are dear to so many Americans, actually lead to physical death.

Abortion and Breast Cancer:
The Deadly Link

Over 1.5 million women abort their babies every year, but what generally is not known by the public is that scientists have found a deadly link between abortion and women who develop breast cancer later in life. There have been over 30 studies that have established this link; however, most Americans are unaware of this deadly link.

Since the 1960s there has been a tremendous increase in the number of women who have been diagnosed with breast cancer. The figures show that 182,000 women each year develop breast cancer and 45,000 will die of the disease, while thousands will suffer both physically and mentally. A woman has a 10 to 12 percent chance of developing breast cancer during her lifetime. At age 45, a woman's risk of developing breast cancer is one percent, and the risk increases until her late seventies when it reaches around 12 percent. What is surprising doctors are the number of women in their late twenties who are now developing breast cancer. With the surge in the breast cancer rate, many doctors are reporting that it has reached a crisis stage.

In November 1994, the National Cancer Institute (NCI) released a study conducted by the Fred Hutchinson Cancer Research Center in Seattle, Washington. The research showed a definite link between abortion and the surge of breast cancer. This research also confirms about 30 previous studies worldwide which have established this deadly link. These studies started in the 1960s, and since the late 1970s this link has been known. Joel Brind, Ph.D., professor of biology and endocrinology at Baruch College of the City College of New York, has been crusading since 1982 to expose the danger of abortion as a major factor in causing breast cancer. Brind tried to get his research out to the public. He blanketed the media with press releases of his findings; however, not one single magazine, newspaper, or news service reported the findings. Brind contacted foreign medical journals, and his research was reported in a British medical journal, *The Lancet.* His article in this journal was read by administrators at Mt. Sinai Medical Center and Beth Israel Hospital, where he held positions as a faculty member and research investigator respectively. As a result of this article, he was immediately fired from both positions. Brind's crusade has been ignored or trivialized by the media and the abortion industry. Is it possible that these studies and Brind's crusade are being ignored so that the killing of children can go on unhindered?

With all the attention given by the medical profession to the cause of breast cancer, and all the money channeled by the government to research, why is the deadly link being ignored? Every conceivable cause of breast cancer has been thoroughly investigated, but the deadly link remains virtually ignored. The natural conclusion is that the abortion–breast cancer link is being ignored because of philosophical reasons. The killing of children in the womb is so important that even the possibility of a deadly consequence is suppressed. Pamela Maraldo of Planned Parenthood (PP) was questioned on November 1, 1994, on NBC's "Dateline" about the results of the NCI research which linked breast cancer and abortion. Maraldo said:

> Even if Dr. Daling's study is solid, good science, then to begin to warn women and upset women on the basis of one study is clearly irresponsible. One study is not adequate evidence . . . to change policy or to upset or frighten women.

Maraldo has to be aware of all the other research that has established the deadly link. If she is not aware of the research, why isn't she demanding additional research to determine if abortion can cause breast cancer in women? Planned Parenthood is the nation's largest abortion provider. PP centers perform over 120,000 abortions on women every year, and yet this organization refuses to even mention to the women that there is a possible link between abortion and breast cancer!! Only a darkened mind would put the killing of children before the health of women!

What the NCI found, and Brind has been trying to tell the public, is that if a woman has an abortion any time during her life, she has increased her chance of developing breast cancer before age 45 by a minimum of 50 percent. The NCI research found that if a woman was under 18 and had an abortion, her risk went to 150 percent. If she was over 30 and had any family history of breast cancer, the risk rocketed to 270 percent. The family history includes mother, sister, grandmother, or even an aunt! The most ominous finding of the study was that *every woman who had an abortion before 18 and had a family history of breast cancer, developed the cancer by the age of 45.* There were just 12 women in the study who fit this criteria; however, all 12 had developed breast cancer.

In December 1993, Howard University released the results of studying 500 black women who had developed breast cancer and had an abortion. The Howard University research found the risk of developing breast cancer before age 40 was 50 percent, which was the same rate found by the National Cancer Institute study. The Howard University research went beyond age 40 to the fifties. The research found that when women who had an abortion passed age 50, they had a much greater chance of developing breast cancer. When the women who had an abortion reached their fifties, the chance of developing breast cancer increased to 370 percent. Study after study is showing this deadly link! Brind found that when the women who have obtained a legal abortion reach age 50, there will be 50,000 additional breast cancer cases every year. Abortion was legalized in 1973, so this huge increase should begin early in the twenty-first century. Brind's calculations were based on a 50 percent increased chance of breast cancer because of an abortion. If the increase risk turns out to be much greater, then as the women pass age 50, this estimate of 50,000 will be too low.

Multiple abortions, in general, greatly increase a woman's chance of developing breast cancer later in life. The more abortions a woman has, the greater the risk. A study in France found that a woman who had a family history of breast cancer and had two or more abortions increased her risk to an incredible 600 percent. In Lithuania it is very common for women to have five abortions by their mid-twenties. Breast cancer is now striking women in their late twenties in that country at an alarming rate. In September 1994, Doctor Valery Ostapenko published an article about breast cancer in Lithuania, and in it said that he "attributes this early onset of the disease to the reproductive system going haywire." Abortion is legal, but it is not a safe procedure. It is deadly to the child, and later to the mother.

Brind found the greatest factor in reducing a woman's chance in developing breast cancer was having a child—especially before age 18. If a woman before age 25 has a child, her risk of developing breast cancer was reduced to 7.5 percent. If a woman aborts her child, she has increased her chance of developing breast cancer by a minimum of 50 percent. If a woman has a 10 percent lifetime chance of developing breast cancer, a 50 percent increase would raise her chance to 15 percent. For the woman who gave birth, the cancer risk was reduced to 7.5 percent. This means a woman who aborts her baby has doubled her breast cancer risk over the woman who gives birth! Every year, approximately 1.5 million women have an abortion. This huge number of women, plus the 10 percent lifetime chance a woman has of developing breast cancer, means that even a slight increase in the breast cancer rate will cause thousands of more women to develop the disease.

The reason abortion causes breast cancer is not known, but Brind believes abortion interrupts the breasts' development and leaves the breast cells in a permanent radical state. When a woman is first pregnant, her body produces large amounts of the hormone estrogen until the ninth week. The estrogen causes dormant cells in the breast to begin maturing to produce milk. After the ninth week, estrogen levels off and gradually decreases until full term. Later in the pregnancy other hormones take over which cause the breast cells to fully mature. Abortion leaves the cells in a permanent suspended state. These cells are neither dormant nor are they mature, and they are the very cells that are susceptible to becoming cancerous. The worst time for a woman to have an abortion is within the first 12 weeks of pregnancy. This is the exact time most abortions occur!

Why, after the 1993 Howard University research and the 1994 National Cancer Institute research, are the main media and medical community so silent about the deadly link? The Cancer Institute's research found every woman who had an abortion before age 18 and had a family history of breast cancer developed the disease. Why has there not been immediate studies following up on this research? The deadly link should be explored to the fullest. It appears, by the silence, that the pro-abortion agenda to kill babies in the womb is more important than the health of women: "All they that hate me [wisdom] love death" (Prov. 8:36).

God's plan is for women to produce life and give birth. God's blessings are connected with a woman conceiving a child: "And God blessed them, and God said unto them, Be fruitful, and multiply" (Gen. 1:28). Children are not a burden, which is the view of so many people today. Children are not to be viewed as wanted or unwanted. Children are not an accident. God has a plan for each child, and children are to be viewed as a blessing: "Lo, children are an heritage of the LORD: and the fruit of the womb is his reward" (Ps. 127:3).

God has designed a woman's body to create life and to produce a child. Her body is extremely fine tuned, and aborting a child is a catastrophic event to her reproductive system. After an abortion, a woman's breasts can literally become cancer time bombs. Abortion defiles the body. The lifestyle that leads to an abortion is one of death. The child is killed immediately, while many mothers die or are physically marred years later. How sad this is. This death and destruction are not God's plan for life, as Jesus said: "I am come that they might have life, and that they might have it more abundantly" (John 10:10).

. . . The End Thereof
Are the Ways of Death

Now, the civil rights battle is for gay rights. Homosexuals are demanding to be accepted as normal, and homosexuality as an accepted alternate lifestyle. Homosexuality is being treated just like abortion rights by the power structure of America. Almost everything Americans are exposed to regarding homosexuality is positive. Even the AMA has adopted a policy of accepting homosexuality as an alternate lifestyle. In December 1994, the AMA took the official position that doctors should not try to discourage homosexuals from their lifestyle. In an official policy statement, the AMA said health care is enhanced by "the physician's non-judgmental recognition of sexual orientation and behavior." Even corporations like AT&T boldly promoted the Gay Olympic Games. There are very few voices warning of the dangers of homosexuality. Homosexuality is being packaged as a basic human right.

The homosexual lifestyle should not be glamorized—it is a lifestyle of death. Most Americans are aware of the high death rate among homosexuals due to AIDS; however, death by AIDS is only a part of the devastation that plagues homosexuals. The Family Research Institute (FRI) has done extensive research into all aspects of homosexuality, including the effect of this lifestyle on their health and life span.

The FRI research found that married women who were never divorced had an average life span of 79 years, and 85 percent lived to be 65 or older. This group had the highest life expectancy. The next highest life expectancy was married men who were never divorced. Their average age at death was 75, with 80 percent living to be 65 or older. The average age of death for unmarried and divorced women dropped to 71, while 60 percent lived to be 65 or older. The average age for single or divorced men dropped to 57, with only 32 percent living to be 65 or older.

The statistics for homosexuals and lesbians are shocking. The average age for homosexuals at death, non-AIDS related, was 42, and only nine percent lived to be 65 or older. If AIDS was the cause of death, the age dropped to 39! Lesbians had a median age of death of 45, and 23 percent lived to be 65 or older (see chart).

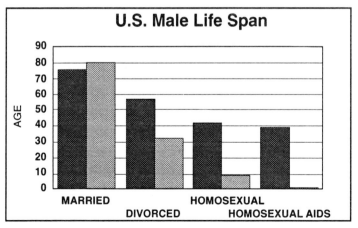

The study found a tremendous amount of violence associated with homosexuality, as 2.9 percent of homosexuals died violently; they were 116 times more likely to be murdered; 24 times more likely to commit suicide; and they were 18 times more likely to die in traffic related accidents than comparably aged white males. Homosexuals had a high rate of death due to heart attacks; cancer and liver failure was exceptionally high. The FRI research finding that the average age of homosexuals dying in their early forties was consistent with scientific literature dating back to 1858. Violence was also associated with lesbianism—22 percent died of murder, suicide, or accident. This rate is 512 times higher than white females aged 25 to 44. Violence and early death are clearly linked with the homosexual lifestyle.

Homosexuals make up about three percent of the population. Although they represent just three percent of the population, as of 1992 eight of the top 10 serial killers in U.S. history were homosexuals. These serial killers follow: Donald Harvey killed 37 in Kentucky; John Wayne Gacy killed 33 young men and boys in Chicago; Patrick Kearney killed 32 in California and then stuffed the bodies in trash bags; Bruce Davis killed 27 young men and boys in Illinois; the homosexual ring of Dean Corll, Elmer Henley, and David Brooks captured, tortured, and killed 27 young men in Texas; Juan Corona killed 25 male migrant workers; Jeffrey Dahmer killed, dismembered, and ate parts of 17 victims in Wisconsin; and Stephen Kraft killed and tortured 16 young men. Special attention has to be given to Gaetan Dugas, who was directly responsible for the death of over 1,000 homosexual men by infecting them with AIDS. Even after he was diagnosed with AIDS, Dugas continued to spread the disease until he died. He was known as "Patient Zero" because he caused so many of the earliest cases of AIDS. The top female serial killer was Aileen Wuornos, a lesbian, who killed seven men. Second place goes to a lesbian nursing team that killed six convalescent patients in Michigan.

A study of serial killers from 1966 to 1983 determined that 19 of the 43 killers (44 percent) were homosexuals. The FRI research found that homosexuals suffered a tremendous rate of venereal disease. Homosexuals are only three percent of the population, yet such murder, death, and disease are directly associated with this lifestyle.

To Dishonor Their Own
Bodies Between Themselves

The issues that are sacred to so many Americans bring death, destruction, and untold misery. The abortion and homosexual lifestyles are lifestyles of death. The power structure of America can make these issues legal and glamorize them but, in the end, they still bring death, destruction, and, ultimately, God's judgment on the nation. The modern "fast lane" lifestyle is a sure road to disease and death. Those who sow abortion and sexual immorality to their bodies, reap death in the end.

Marriage between a man and a woman was the very first institution that God created: "Therefore shall a man . . . cleave unto his wife: and they shall be one flesh" (Gen. 2:24). God blessed this union and the children that it produces: "And God blessed them, and God said unto them, Be fruitful, and multiply . . ." (Gen. 1:28). The Bible clearly states there are blessings, including long life, for those that obey God's Word: "My son, forget not my law; but let thine heart keep my commandments: For length of days, *and long life*, and peace, shall they add to thee" (Prov. 3:1–2). The FRI research just confirms the promise of the Bible. *Men and women who were married only once were the people with the longest life span.* To those who do not live by God's principles, disease

160—God's Final Warning to America

and an early death await: "Be not deceived; God is not mocked: for whatsoever a man soweth, that shall he also reap" (Gal. 6:7).

Prior to 1962 every state had criminal laws against homosexuality. As prayer and God's Word were removed from the nation's schools, the states began to rescind the laws against homosexuality. By the 1990s, only 19 states had laws against homosexuality, and these laws are seldom enforced. As God's Word was being removed from America, it is no coincidence that homosexuality and abortion began to proliferate. The removal of God's Word has brought death and destruction. There are hundreds of thousands of Americans infected with AIDS. Tens of thousands die each year, and 65 to 70 percent will be homosexuals. Each year, thousands of homosexuals will die young due to "natural causes." The homosexual lifestyle is one of death. Over 1.5 million babies die each year from abortion, and based on statistics it is possible that 10,000 women a year die from breast cancer caused by these abortions. Tens of thousands of other women will be disfigured and suffer emotional scars because of abortion-related breast cancer.

Breast cancer is to abortion as AIDS is to homosexuality. This can be seen in San Francisco. This city is known as the homosexual "capital of the world," and also quite possibly the AIDS capital of the United States. The "fast life" has caught up with San Francisco's women. In December 1994, Dr. Robert Hiatt of the Northern California Cancer Center said that "white women living in the San Francisco Bay area have the highest rate of breast cancer in the world." San Francisco is now known as the AIDS and breast cancer capital of the world. What are the medical costs for all the AIDS patient care and breast cancer treatment? What about the emotional scars women suffer and carry because they have killed their child in their own womb? These lifestyles have cost Americans billions of dollars.

God Gave Them Over to a Reprobate Mind

The *Random House College Dictionary* defines reprobate as "a depraved, unprincipled, or wicked person or morally depraved; unprincipled; bad." The Bible devotes an entire chapter to identifying a reprobate, describing how a person becomes a reprobate, and the judgment for being a reprobate.

The first chapter of Romans gives God's view of a reprobate. The first step in becoming a reprobate is the failure to acknowledge God: "Because that, when they knew God, they glorified him not as God, neither were thankful; but became vain in their imaginations, and their foolish heart was darkened" (vs. 21). This is followed by denying the truth of God and His Word and believing lies: "Who changed the truth of God into a lie" (vs. 25). Following the living of a lie, the presence of God departs from a person's life, leaving a huge void. This void is filled by turning to sexual immorality and ending with homosexuality:

> For this cause God gave them up unto vile affections: for even their women did change the natural use into that which is against nature: And likewise also the men, leaving the natural use of the women, burned in their lust one toward another.
>
> —vss. 26–27

When a person lives a lie, he drives the knowledge of God out of his mind and becomes a reprobate: "And even as they did not like to retain God in their knowledge, God gave them over to a reprobate mind, to do those things which are not convenient" (vs. 28).

The explosion in America of pornography, lewd movies, fornication, adultery, divorce, and homosexuality are all clear signs that the nation has become reprobate before God. The acceptance and promotion of homosexuality as being an alternate lifestyle is the key sign, and the "end of the road" to being a reprobate. To God, those that give consent that sexual immorality is an alternate lifestyle are as guilty as those who live the lifestyle. They also are reprobates: "Not only do the same, but have pleasure in them that do them" (vs. 32). The words "have pleasure" in this verse means, "to consent with them."

Following the identification of a reprobate, the Bible lists 23 characteristics of what happens when a reprobate mind takes hold of people. Some of the characteristics are *fornication, murder, envy, haters of God, without natural affection, and deceit* (Rom. 1:29–31). Two of these characteristics of being a reprobate are so fitting for America and the abortion mentality. They are *unmerciful* and *inventors of evil things*.

How a reprobate mind of being *unmerciful* and an *inventor of evil things* has taken hold of America can easily be seen in the medical profession. On September 13–14, 1992, the National Abortion Federation held a seminar in Dallas, Texas, to advance late-term abortions in America. The seminar was titled "Risk Management Seminar—Second Trimester Abortion: From Every Angle." One of the speakers was Dr. Martin Haskell, who owns abortion centers in Cincinnati and Dayton, Ohio. His topic was titled "Second Trimester D&X, 20 Weeks and Beyond." *D&X* was the title Dr. Haskell coined for a technique that he had invented to abort late-term babies. *D&X* stands for "dilation and extraction." Dilation is for the cervix, and extraction is for the removal of the baby from the mother. Dr. Haskell said he uses this abortion technique on babies 20 to 26 weeks gestation. He admitted performing over 1,000 of these D&X-type abortions. Technically, what Dr. Haskell is doing is not an abortion. The *Random House College Dictionary* defines abortion as "the expulsion of a human fetus within the first twelve weeks of pregnancy, before it is viable." Actually, Dr. Haskell is committing infanticide!

During his presentation, Dr. Haskell explained in detail the technique of a D&X abortion. (The series of drawings below explains the D&X technique.) A review of Dr. Haskell's paper, which he presented at the seminar, revealed the D&X procedure starts by using ultrasound to locate the baby. A large grasping forceps is inserted and grasps the babies lower extremity. The baby is then pulled down the birth canal until the surgeon can place his fingers on the baby's shoulders. The rest is best explained by Dr. Haskell himself directly from his paper:

While maintaining this tension, lifting the cervix and applying traction to the shoulders with the fingers of the

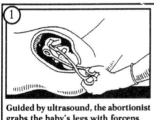

Guided by ultrasound, the abortionist grabs the baby's legs with forceps

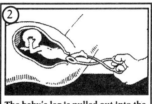

The baby's leg is pulled out into the birth canal.

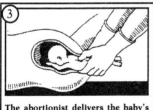

The abortionist delivers the baby's entire body, except for the head.

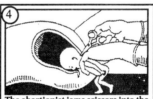

The abortionist jams scissors into the baby's skull. The scissors are then opened to enlarge the hole

The scissors are removed and a suction catheter is inserted. The child's brains are sucked out. The baby is then "evacuated."

> left hand, the surgeon takes a pair of blunt curved scissors
> in the right hand. He carefully advances the tip, curved
> down, along the spine and under his middle finger until
> he feels it contact the base of the skull under the tip of
> his middle finger. . . . The surgeon then forces the scissors
> into the base of the skull. . . . Having safely entered the
> skull, he spreads the scissors to enlarge the opening. The
> surgeon removes the scissors and introduces a suction
> catheter into this hole and evacuates the skull contents.
> With the catheter still in place, he applies traction to the
> fetus, removing it completely from the patient.

Because the baby was not fully delivered from the mother,
this is a legal "abortion" and not infanticide. The baby can
be killed by the D&X method because about 80 to 90 percent of the skull remains in the mother. This procedure is
legal by the mere two or three inches of the baby that remains in the mother!

The horror of the D&X abortion method reached the
Congress of the U.S. Both the House and Senate held hearings. The D&X procedure was formally titled "partial-birth
abortion." The hearing revealed the truth surrounding this
procedure. The hearings revealed that 80 percent of these
aborted babies were perfectly healthy. The partial-birth
procedure killed the baby. Many of these little babies were
capable of living on their own. The procedure was not done
as an emergency to save the life of the mother, because it
takes three days to complete. The partial-birth procedure
is simply to kill a little child in the womb.

Brenda Shafer, RN, worked for a brief period for Dr.
Haskell. She witnessed several partial-birth abortions. In a
letter to Congressman Tony Hall she brought to light what
actually happened. In the letter she said:

> As Dr. Haskell watched the baby on the ultrasound screen,
> he went in with the forceps and grabbed the baby's legs

and brought them down into the birth canal. Then he delivered the body and arms, all the way up to the neck. At this point, only the baby's head was still inside. The baby's body was moving. His little fingers were clasping together. He was kicking his feet. All the while his little head was still stuck inside. Dr. Haskell took a pair of scissors and inserted them into the back of the baby's head. Then he opened the scissors up. Then he stuck the high-powered suction tube into the hole and sucked the baby's brains out. I almost threw up as I watched him do these things. . . . I still have nightmares about what I saw.

The House and Senate passed legislation to ban the partial–birth abortion procedure. An exception was made to save the life of the mother. The ban included felony charges against any doctor who performed this procedure. On April 10, 1996, President Clinton vetoed the legislation. He vetoed the ban a second time on October 10, 1997. The president felt politically secure enough to twice veto the ban. How sad for America, when the horror of the partial-birth abortion procedure was exposed, there was not enough pressure from the public to have it banned.

The Bible states that a reprobate mind invents evil things, and the D&X abortion technique is a perfect example. Only a reprobate mind could invent such a gruesome technique; or the vacuum machine used in early abortions to suck the baby out of the mother: or the pill, RU-486, which a woman takes to cause an abortion.

The medical profession, with its pro-abortion position, stands behind this procedure. Some doctors may not endorse the D&X procedure, but the profession cannot stop it. The legal profession, with its pro-abortion position, stands behind this procedure. The courts have made abortion a "constitutional right" and will do nothing to protect a full-term child from such a gruesome death.

If pro-life protesters try to protect the child, the police will use all the force necessary to ensure that the doctor can use the D&X procedure. Even some mothers and fathers will allow this procedure to be done to their own flesh and blood. This procedure is completely legal! Until the procedure is illegal, it is a witness to the reprobate nature of America. The babies receive no mercy from any segment of American society. This is the end result of rejecting God, living lies, and the ensuing reprobate mind.

When confronted with the horrors of the D&X procedure, pro-abortion forces claimed the babies were already dead before the skull was crushed open and the brains removed. When Dr. Haskell admitted the babies were alive, the pro-abortion forces tried to minimize the horror by claiming "only" 400 to 500 babies were "aborted" this way a year. Approximately 13,000 babies a year are aborted in the third trimester; but even if only 400 to 500 are killed this way, what have we become as a nation to allow and protect the destruction of babies in the womb by the D&X procedure. Are Americans so reprobate as a nation that the death of a "small" number of babies by the D&X procedure does not matter?

America as a nation is a long way down the road to developing a reprobate, national consensus. In 1963, America turned from God, and since then the knowledge of God has been systematically removed from all areas of our society. In direct proportion to the removal of the knowledge of God has been the acceptance of fornication and adultery, and the promotion of homosexuality and child killing. The media and Hollywood glorify these lifestyles. The courts have established them as "rights." The college campuses are a fertile ground for these lifestyles. Even political parties promote them.

It seems the collective thought of America is now almost very close to being reprobate. As the nation has turned from God, multitudes of people now live lies and America has become nearly reprobate. This has happened in a very short time. Let no one try to fool you. If a person accepts or promotes homosexuality and/or abortion, to God they are a reprobate. The education, position of power, social standing (including position of religious authority), or wealth, does not matter to God. They are reprobate. America has many reprobates in very powerful positions of authority.

There appears to be no letup from those of a reprobate mind to promote these deadly lifestyles. To those who promote these "deathstyles," these issues have become like a religion. Abortion and homosexuality look so normal to a reprobate mind. Following God's Word brings blessings, health, and long life; following the reprobate mind brings disease, death, and destruction.

How can Americans sit back and let their children be taught that these lifestyles are "rights" when they lead directly to disease, misery, and death? How can Americans sit back and let their tax money be used to promote, support, encourage, and pay for these lifestyles! Americans, as they have rejected God's Word, are being led like sheep to the slaughter. There are no standards for Americans to live by. Slogans such as, "pro-choice," "it's my body," "it's just a fetus," "reproductive freedom," and "civil rights–gay rights" have swayed millions of Americans. This mindless thinking has brought death and destruction to America and an awesome collision course with God.

> I call heaven and earth to record this day against you, that I have set before you life and death, blessing and cursing: therefore choose life, that both thou and thy seed may live.
> —Deuteronomy 30:19

Chapter Six

America:
My People Know Not the
Judgment of the Lord

God always warns a nation before judgment. God is extremely merciful and very slow to anger, but there is a point when He will move to punish. The punishment could mean the total destruction of a nation or empire. The Bible records the destruction of God's ancient Jewish people and their removal from the land of Israel in 600 B.C. For two centuries before the destruction, God sent prophet after prophet to warn Israel of the coming disaster. The people for the most part refused to turn from sin. The result was that multitudes died as the country was destroyed and the survivors were taken captive to Babylon.

The prophet Jeremiah was alive when Israel was destroyed. He warned of the coming destruction and pleaded with Israel to turn to God. The people would not listen to his warning. Jeremiah wept over his people, and today he is known as the weeping prophet. When the people failed to recognize that the calamities coming on them were warnings from God of impending destruction, Jeremiah said, "My people know not the judgment of the LORD" (Jer. 8:7).

Modern America is very similar to ancient Israel. Both nations were founded for the glory of God and have a godly heritage. Both nations turned from God and went into gross sexual immorality while yet still appearing to remain religious. Both nations practiced child killing, and tolerated, if not encouraged, open homosexuality. Just before destruction, both nations were consumed with violence. And both nations were clearly warned by God of the coming destruction.

When the Supreme Court in 1963 banned prayer and Bible reading in the public schools, and then in 1973 legalized the killing of innocent children in the womb, the country was destabilized. It is now clear that judgment from God began in 1963 and was intensified in 1973.

Since 1963 the education system, once the best in the world, is now second rate. The family unit through adultery, divorce, and violence is disintegrating. The cities are now drug infested war zones. Our children are abused and sexually molested. Homosexuals parade openly in the streets, and vile pornographers degrade women and children and make millions of dollars. Sexual immorality has brought with it AIDS, which is the deadliest disease known to mankind. The American government is trillions of dollars in debt. America cannot continue in this direction and be a great nation: "Righteousness exalteth a nation: but sin is a reproach to any people" (Prov. 14:34). Remember, the Index of Social Health has pinpointed *1973* as the very year the deterioration of America began.

The Bible states: "If the foundations be destroyed, what can the righteous do?" (Ps. 11:3). The foundations of America have been destroyed. The husband and wife family unit, which is ordained by God, is being replaced with the term "domestic partners," and homosexuals are being allowed to adopt children. America has become unglued! The nation is full of violence as innocent blood is being shed from coast to coast. It seems every week a mass murderer kills several people. This was unheard of before 1963. It seems that regularly a serial killer is caught, and these killers are more and more bizarre. This was virtually unheard of before 1963. The violence which started against children in the womb has now spread like a cancer throughout the entire society. It is truly ironic that America has developed the technology to allow men to walk safely in space, yet most of our cities' streets are now unsafe to walk in.

Most Americans know something is radically wrong with the country, only they do not know the cause. They blame the courts, schools, the economy, or politicians, but the real problem is, as a nation, America has rejected God. Like ancient Israel, Americans have failed to see that national calamities are warnings of impending destruction.

The fourth and eighth greatest earthquakes this century occurring on the very morning of Gay Pride Day should have had the entire nation's attention. These earthquakes shook huge sections of the West Coast, but hardly anyone seems to connect this and the other calamities with God: "My people know not the judgment of the Lord."

For the Wages of Sin Is Death

Sin is rebellion against God and His Word. The mere mention of the word sin brings a mocking from many Americans. Sin is nothing to laugh at, but the practice of sin brings dire consequences to individuals, families, institutions, and nations. Sin has been dressed up to the point that alcoholism and drug addiction are now a "disease." Fornication is called being "sexually active." Adultery is now an "extramarital affair." Pornography is given the innocent sounding title of "adult entertainment." Homosexuality is an "alternate lifestyle," while abortion is just a "simple" medical procedure. There is very little stigma attached to those who practice sin. The government has even ruled that killing children in the womb is a "constitutional right," and homosexuality is being dealt with as a "fundamental" civil rights issue.

The Bible is clear that the breaking of God's law will lead to the destruction of those who practice it: "Then when lust hath conceived, it bringeth forth sin: and sin, when it is finished, bringeth forth death" (James 1:15).

Sin is no laughing matter. Sin is the cause of what is destroying this once great nation. America is starting to buckle under the weight of the multitude of people who are living destructive and sinful lifestyles.

Sin brings with it physical death to those who practice it. Alcoholism, drug addiction, and sexual diseases have prematurely destroyed multitudes. Sin brings death to children as Americans abort 1.5 million babies a year. How many babies were aborted because of the sins of fornication, adultery, divorce, incest, rape, and pornography?

Sin destroys families. Alcohol, drugs, adultery, and pornography have all contributed to destroying families through violence and divorce. The broken families lead directly to the destruction of institutions such as the welfare, school, and penal systems. The children from broken families bring severe problems into the schools, and these children do not learn as well as children from stable homes. Many youngsters from broken families end up in trouble with the law, and so many youths are now involved in the courts that the legal system has broken down. Much of the violence in America can be traced to the breakdown of the family unit. If enough Americans are living sinful lifestyles, it will literally bring death to all the institutions, and then death to the nation. Sin costs Americans tens of billions of dollars every year.

The progression of sin is first the destruction of the person; then the family; then the institutions; and then the nation itself: "For the wages of sin is death" (Rom. 6:23).

Sin has progressed to such a state in America since 1963 that the very foundation of America is now at stake.

The former Soviet Union and the Eastern European countries are good examples of what happens to nations that reject God and lead godless lives. America is fast heading in this direction. Large numbers of Americans now lead lifestyles which are directly causing the destruction of the country: "There is a way that seemeth right unto a man, but the end thereof are the ways of death" (Prov. 16:25).

For I Am the Lord: I Change Not

Modern Americans have a very strange view of God and faith. The prevailing view is that God is whatever a person wants Him to be, and as long as that person is sincere, his or her faith is good. Some believe God is a cosmic force, while others believe God is impersonal. The Bible states: "They that worship him must worship in spirit and truth" (John 4:24). We are not to pick and choose what to believe, but seek the objective truth about the person of God. God has revealed the truth about Himself in the Bible.

The very nature of God is holiness. This is the very core of God. God's holiness is what separates sinful mankind from Him. Man is alienated from God because of sin. God deals with man in absolutes, and the breaking of God's laws is called sin. Multitudes of Americans now reject the mere thought of absolutes; however, these people still hold to one absolute—that there are absolutely no absolutes. The rejection of God and His absolutes is causing the destruction of America.

God is very merciful and desires that no one be separated from Him, "but is longsuffering to us-ward, not willing that any should perish, but that all should *come to repentance*" (2 Pet. 3:9). God truly loves man and wants fellowship with man. Through Jesus Christ God's love reached out to mankind to restore the fellowship that was broken by man's sin.

Although God is very merciful and loves man, His holiness will not allow such sin as the killing of innocent children in the womb to go without punishment. God would cease to be God if He did not act. God will warn in a variety of ways over a period of time, but at some point He will move in judgment. America is now at that threshold.

The sin of America has offended God's holiness, and He is now moving to confront America's sin. In the past God was the friend of America, but today America has become the enemy of God. America is approaching the last innocent child in the womb that God's patience and mercy will allow to be killed.

If My People Turn from Their Wicked Ways

The cataclysmic disasters and social deterioration should have the attention of every Christian in America. The awesome earthquakes on abortion/homosexual related events should have opened the eyes of every Christian that God is about to judge the nation for sin. There are a core of Christians that are standing for righteousness and are aware of the impending judgment. Unfortunately, there seems to be a spiritual dullness over the majority of God's people.

Many view abortion, homosexuality, and other sins as political issues. Far too many preachers and church leaders have been silent and have not alerted the people to the reality of the state of America before God. Many Christians have lost the true fear of God and the awesomeness of His holiness. The result of all this is a lack of zeal to confront the crisis America faces. America is running headlong into a confrontation with God, and a great part of the church remains silent.

Gay Pride Day should be a national day of fasting, prayer, and humiliation before God. The churches should be packed with people interceding before God. Abortion related events should cause millions of Christians to cry out to God for mercy on the land. There should be hundreds and hundreds of Christians in front of the abortion centers on a regular basis praying and crying out to God because His children are being killed. The reason to go to the centers is to repent, pray for God to move in America, and intercede before God for the life of the child. The purpose of going to the abortion centers is to intercede before God and not to make a political statement.

Where are God's people in this hour of crisis? Where are the leaders of the church? God wants His people to stand: "Who will rise up for me against the evildoers? or who will stand up for me against the workers of iniquity?" We are to stand specifically against those that shed innocent blood: "They gather themselves together against the soul of the righteous, and condemn the innocent blood" (Ps. 94:21). The church brings glory to God by standing for righteousness. Because of the sin of America, it seems the church has been desensitized and now lacks the resolve to stand. God's attitude toward sexual sin and child killing is the same today as it was in the days of Sodom and Gomorrah.

America is beyond being saved by politics, education, or social action. America needs God to move in peoples lives, breaking the hold that destructive sinful lifestyles have over them. God is not going to move until His people, first in true repentance and in humility, cry out to Him:

> If my people, which are called by my name, shall *humble* themselves, and pray, and seek my face, and *turn from their wicked ways;* then will I hear from heaven, and will forgive their sin, and will heal their land.
>
> —2 Chronicles 7:14

The church in America is not humble before God and has

to truly repent of the sin which is in the church and the nation. God is waiting on His people. Are we going to stop playing church and focus on what God's Word says?

The Gift of God Is Eternal Life

America is in trouble because multitudes of people have turned away from God and are not living according to His Word. It is the corporate effect of individual people which is destroying America. The country is being destroyed individual by individual, and to be restored it has to be done individual by individual. Not only does sin destroy lives, it also destroys lives eternally by separating people from God. In eternity there is a literal heaven and a literal hell.

God's answer for restoring the nation is through the life-changing power of the gospel of Jesus Christ, and then having people live according to His Word. The life–changing power of the gospel is awesome and will break all sinful lifestyles:

> Know ye not that the unrighteous shall not inherit the kingdom of God? Be not deceived: neither fornicators, nor idolaters, nor adulterers, nor effeminate, nor abusers of themselves with mankind, Nor thieves, nor covetous, nor drunkards, nor revilers, nor extortioners, shall inherit the kingdom of God. And such were some of you: but ye are washed, but ye are sanctified, but ye are justified in the name of the Lord Jesus, and by the Spirit of our God.
> —1 Corinthians 6:9–11

Notice in this Bible verse that after a list of destructive lifestyles, the verse goes on to say the believers have been washed, sanctified, and justified. The Bible is clear that no matter what a person's present lifestyle is, or what a person did in the past, they can be forgiven. A new life can be started in Jesus Christ.

When the Lord Jesus died on the cross, His death and shed blood paid the complete price for sin. Because of the shed blood of Christ, everyone can be reconciled with God: "In whom we have redemption through his blood, even the forgiveness of sins" (Col. 1:14). Through faith in Christ all guilt can be removed, and you can have peace in your life: "Therefore being justified by faith, we have peace with God through our Lord Jesus Christ" (Rom. 5:1).

When Jesus Christ rose from the dead, He rose with power. The resurrection power of Christ is the power of God that breaks the hold that sinful lifestyles have on people. Through faith in Jesus Christ a person can have total assurance of eternal life with God: "These things have I written unto you that believe on the name of the Son of God; that ye may know that ye have eternal life, and that ye may believe on the name of the Son of God" (1 John 5:13).

The Irony of Redemption

God literally hates the shedding of innocent blood: "These . . . things doth the LORD hate . . . hands that shed innocent blood" (Prov. 6: 16–17). From the first book of the Bible, Genesis, to the last book, Revelation, God is clear that the shedding of innocent blood is awesome to Him.

In the book of Genesis, God told Cain after he had slain his brother: "What hast thou done? the voice of thy brother's blood crieth unto me from the ground" (Gen. 4:10). The book of Revelation records God's awesome judgments on the earth for sin, just before the second coming of Jesus Christ. In the midst of the judgment the Bible states:

> Thou art righteous, O Lord, which art, and wast, and shalt be, because thou hast judged thus. For they have shed the blood of saints and prophets, and thou hast given them blood to drink; for they are worthy.
>
> —Revelation 16:5–6

To secure man's redemption, Jesus Christ had to endure what God hates. The innocent blood of Christ, the Son of God, was shed to pay the penalty for sin. God allowed His Son's blood to be shed so that sinful man could be redeemed! The gospel of Jesus Christ is not to be trivialized. Christ paid the ultimate price—His innocent blood was shed. It is truly ironic that the shed blood of Christ pays the penalty for those who shed the blood of children in the womb. To those who trust Jesus Christ as their Savior, sin is forgiven— even the sin of killing innocent children in the womb.

The importance of the shed blood of Jesus Christ can be seen in the Bible verses which follow: "Unto him that loved us, and washed us from our sins in his own blood" (Rev. 1:5). "For thou wast slain, and hast redeemed us to God by thy blood out of every kindred, and tongue, and people, and nation" (Rev. 5:9).

Conclusion

The prophet Isaiah, 2,700 years ago, confronted the sin of ancient Israel with a message of hope from God. This same message is desperately needed to be heard by modern Americans. Isaiah said:

> Come now, and let us reason together, saith the LORD: though your sins be as scarlet, they shall be as white as snow; though they be red like crimson, they shall be as wool.
>
> —Isaiah 1:18

God has provided a way to deal with man's sinful lifestyle, and that is through repentance and completely trusting in Jesus Christ for salvation. Repentance is an act of the will and involves cutting the ties with the old way of life. Repentance from a destructive lifestyle, including materialism, is absolutely necessary to be forgiven by God. Americans are being destroyed by sin. God is waiting to forgive and heal: "For the wages of sin is death; but the gift of God is eternal life through Jesus Christ our Lord" (Rom. 6:23)

America is fast approaching the last innocent child in the womb to be killed; the last child to be molested or abused; the last Gay Pride Day; the last vile pornographic book, magazine, or movie to be made; the last act of adultery; the last divorce; the last violent crime; the last drug deal; and the last lie to be told to our youth by such groups as Planned Parenthood. America is rushing headlong into a confrontation with God.

In the past, Americans honored God and His Word, and God greatly blessed the country. Today, America is the enemy of God. Many Americans still have an appearance of religion, but their heart is gone astray from God. True faith in Jesus Christ will put the resolve back in Americans that is needed to stand against the forces which are destroying this once great nation. Honoring God's Word is the anchor of truth that Americans desperately need.

If God destroyed America tomorrow, He could not be accused of being harsh. His patience has allowed numerous Gay Pride Days and over 30 million babies to be killed. America has been fully warned.

God has warned in the Bible that He will destroy nations for the sin America is now practicing and condoning. He has warned through those who stand for righteousness. This would include the various aspects of the pro-life movement. He has warned through awesome natural disasters that have coincided with abortion/homosexual related events. God truly loves America, but the unrepentant sin of America demands that He must judge.

My heart's desire is that the church of Jesus Christ will awaken, and spiritual life and power from God's Holy Spirit will come into it. This awakening of the church will then spread to the entire country and multitudes will turn to

Jesus Christ from destructive and sinful lifestyles. My heart's desire is that America will stop the wholesale slaughter of innocent children in the womb. My heart's desire is that America will repent of this course of national suicide and confrontation with the living God, and judgment will be stayed. Judgment will only be stayed as individuals like yourself turn to Jesus Christ and live with resolve according to His Word.

> But the fearful, and unbelieving, and the abominable, and murderers, and whoremongers, and sorcerers, and idolaters, and all liars, shall have their part in the lake which burneth with fire and brimstone: which is the second death.
>
> —Revelation 21:8

> That if thou shalt confess with thy mouth the Lord Jesus, and shalt believe in thine heart that God hath raised him from the dead, thou shalt be saved. For with the heart man believeth unto righteousness; and with the mouth confession is made unto salvation.
>
> —Romans 10:9–10

National Prayer for Life

Mr. Brennan was inspired to write this poem on the way home after attending the January 22, 1992, annual *March for Life* in Washington, D.C.

> We came forth from many quarters,
>   one hundred thousand strong,
>   to focus our nation's conscience
>   on a gross and serious wrong.
> Nearly thirty million children
>   were aborted from the womb,
>   a plastic bag their only shroud,
>   a garbage can their tomb.
> No comrades fought on either flank
>   no sword or shield did fend.
> Their nation left them on their own.
> Alone they met their end.
>
> No caisson bore them to their grave,
>   less friends and floral too.
> For them no flag was flown half-mast.
> For them no bugle blew.
> We weep for this our nation,
>   which feeds upon its youth,
>   for its eyes are sadly blinded
>   to equality and truth.
> We pray for this our nation:
> May this bloody slaughter cease,
>   so our God who gave it freedom
>   may restore to it His peace.

Signs of the Times

by Kathleen Chatters

Destruction is coming, but we do not see;
Because we have chosen to live selfishly.
But church wake up; the end draweth nigh!
Our Lord God is speaking to both you and I!

The signs of the times are so plain to see.
Stop, look, and listen is my urgent plea.
God, our Father has work to be done;
The same work as Jesus, His Son.

Rise up, get busy; we haven't much time
To get things in order; It's your job and mine.
It's not our will but Thy will be done.
So pray to our Father in the Name of His Son.

He'll show us the fields where He wants us to work.
If we study His Word and just stay alert.
The harvest is plenty, the laborers few.
So work while it's light before dark is upon you.

We go to a building and call it our church.
But we are the church not doing God's work!
We sing and we dance and we shout, "Praise the Lord!"
With blind eyes and deaf ears not heeding His Word.

We say we love Jesus and we are His bride.
But we haven't submitted to the Word, our Guide.
We pray, "Lord, please bless me and make it all right!"
Thinking just of ourselves and not the world's plight.

We must be transformed with a mind that's renewed.
Thinking on Him and the work we're to do.
Pray, "Lord, change me," and then things will change.
And God will be pleased when we honor His Name.

Look at this world and study His Word,
Using spiritual eyes so our vision's not blurred.
Listen with spiritual ears for God's truth;
Being one in His Spirit so His Word will be proved.

We live in a world where "wrong" is called "right."
We're deceived in our minds, saying, "It's not my fight!"
So millions of babies continue to die.
We have men loving men, and we call it gay pride!

God is not silent, nor is He pleased.
Look at His warnings for you and for me.
He wants our attention before it's too late.
The signs of the times are sealing our fate.

God is not slack in His promises made.
With longsuffering and patience He waits like He said.
But time is short, and time is running out;
Fighting sin, winning souls is what we're about.

Israel is not just some land over there.
It's Gods covenant land to be lifted in prayer.
Pray it be blessed and our blessings be sure;
For nations that curse it will never endure.

Jerusalem is God's most holy place,
Forever a gift for God's holy race.
"Forever" was spoken by God and not man.
It's foolish to think we could change what He planned.

There's homeless to feed and prisoners to see,
Reaching out to our neighbors and hurt families.
Training our children the way they should go
Based on God's Word they'll be nourished and grow.

Can two walk together except they're agreed?
Agree with God's Word and He'll intercede.
He hates the shedding of innocent blood,
And this sin in our nation has come like a flood.

The love of money is the root of all evil
And abortionists thrive on the babies they kill.
So fast and pray for these precious small souls
Made in God's image with a will He controls.

For each has a purpose, for each He a plan;
Created for God and not will of man.
Satan has come to steal, kill, and destroy.
So we cast out our babies like some broken toy.

It's a serious church issue, and we can't just ignore,
There's work for us all; of this to be sure!
God told us to stand for His righteousness;
To live holy so we be a nation that's blessed.

God called His people to be humble and pray
And turn from our sins; there's no other way.
For if we will do just as He has planned,
He'll forgive us our sins and then heal our land.

If we do what He says and we pray without ceasing,
Our victory's sure and it's God we'll be pleasing.
He gave all His angels charge over His saints;
It's all perfect wisdom without any restraints.

The floods, hurricanes, earthquakes, and tornadoes,
Stock market crashes, and fires all tell us
God's warning His people to fast and to pray.
We must do it "NOW" before God's Judgment Day.

Lack of His Knowledge will bring us destruction.
So love our God first, and heed His instruction.
And pay close attention to signs of the times,
Rejoicing as onward and upward we climb!

Documentation

Chapter One

Billion Dollar Disasters

Report dated June 11, 1997, from the National Climatic Data Center, Asheville, NC. Report titled "Billion Dollar U.S. Weather Disasters 1980–1997."

October 1987

Homosexual march on Washington: *New York Times*, October 12, 1987, front page article titled "200,000 March in Capital to Seek Gay Rights and Money for AIDS"; *Washington Post*, October 12, 1987, front page article titled "Hundreds of Thousands March for Gay Rights"; and *The Patriot-News*, Harrisburg, PA, October 12, 1987, article titled "200,000 March in Washington for Gay Causes."

Stock market: *New York Times*, October 17, 1987, front page article titled "Stock Prices Fall on a Broad Front; Volume is Record"; *The Patriot-News*, October 20, 1987, front page article titled "Market Fall Rivals '29 Crash."

Chart: *New York Times*, February 14, 1993, article titled "The Week of the Economy."

Stock market not recovered by 1992: *USA Today*, August 26, 1992, article titled "Market Still Feels Tremors of '87 Crash."

September 1989

Hurricane Hugo: Headline article, *Washington Post*, September 21, 1989, front page article titled "Troops Ordered to Calm Virgin Islands (Looting Continues; Hurricane Expected to Hit Mainland Friday)"; *USA Today*, September 22, 1989, front page article titled "Monster Hugo Surges Ashore."

Abortion and Supreme Court: *Washington Post*, September 21, 1989, front page article titled "U.S. May Forego Request for Abortion Review (Administration Faces Friday Deadline for Action in Minnesota Case)."

October 1989

Pro-abortion activity: *The Patriot-News*, Harrisburg, PA, October 12, 1989, front page articles titled "House Widens U.S. Funding for Abortion" and "Florida Refuses Abortion Restrictions."

Stock market: *The Patriot-News*, October 14, 1989, front page article titled "Market Takes New Plunge: 190 Points"

Ten governor's pro-abortion statement: *The Patriot-News*, October 16, 1989, page A3, article titled "Ten Governors Urge High Court to Uphold Abortion Rights."

Pro-abortion rally in San Francisco: *San Francisco Chronicle*, October 16,

1989, front page article titled "A Huge, Spirited Abortion-Rights Rally in S.F."

Earthquake: *The Patriot-News*, October 18, 1989, front page article titled "Quake Kills 47 in California."

April 1992

Pro-abortion march: *Washington Post*, April 6, 1992, front page article titled "Abortion-Rights Rally Draws Half a Million Marchers."

Operation Rescue Buffalo: *USA Today*, April 21, 1992, page 3A, article titled "Face-Off in Buffalo."

Supreme Court hearing / earthquake: *The Patriot (Evening News)*, Harrisburg, PA, April 23, 1992, front page articles titled "Justices Begin Review of State Abortion Law" and "Strong Quake Rattles West."

Counter protest / earthquake: *The Philadelphia Inquirer*, April 26, 1992, front page article titled "Quake Rocks N. Calif," and page A4 article titled "Abortion Clash at Buffalo Clinic"; *The Wanderer*, St. Paul, MN, May 7, 1992, article titled "Jaws of Hell Open Wide in Buffalo."

End of Operation Rescue Buffalo / jury decision: *USA Today*, April 21, 1992, page 3A, article titled "King Case May Go To Jury Today in L.A."; *New York Times*, April 30, 1992, front page articles titled "Los Angeles Policemen Acquitted in Taped Beating" and "Down and Divided in Buffalo, Abortion Foes Suspend Siege"; *New York Times*, May 1, 1992, front page article titled "11 Dead in Los Angeles Rioting; 4,000 Guard Troops Called Out as Fires and Looting Continue."

June 1992

Landers quake triggers quakes throughout West: "Lessons From Landers" by Richard Monastersky, *Earth Magazine*, March 1993, pages 41-47 and "Learning from the Whispers" by Larry J. Ruff, *Nature Magazine*, vol. 364, August 12, 1993, pages 567–576.

"Gay Pride Day" / earthquake: *Los Angeles Times*, June 29, 1992, front page articles titled "2 Strong Quakes Jolt Wide Area" and "200,000 Attend Gay Pride Parade."

Supreme Court decision / earthquake: *USA Today*, June 30, 1992, front page articles titled "Future of 'Roe' Hangs by One Vote" and "Californians Warned of More Quakes Ahead."

Connection between April 23–June 28, 1992, earthquakes: *Los Angeles Times*, January 20, 1994, article titled "Scientists Ponder Northward Concentration of Quakes."

March 1993

Oregon Medicaid plan: *USA Today*, March 19, 1993, article titled "Oregon Expects OK for Medicaid-Rationing Plan."

Salem earthquake: *USA Today*, March 26, 1993, article titled "Northwest Jolted Into Reality."

Health plan goes into effect: *USA Today*, February 2, 1994, page 3, article titled "Oregon Health Plan."

June 1993

"Gay Pride Day" 1993: *San Francisco Chronicle*, June 28, 1993, article titled "Gay Parade Celebrates a Breakout Year"

Shipping stopped on June 25: *Philadelphia Inquirer*, July 11, 1993, page A5, article titled "Misery Flows from River Now."

Flood started on Gay Pride Day: *USA Today*, July 8, 1993, article titled "Spring Sprinkles, Summer Surge" and August 2, 1993, front page article titled "City Under Attack; River 'Won't Let Go.'"

Results of flood: *USA Today*, unknown date, article titled "The Great Flood of '93."

July 1993

Operation Rescue / "Cities of Refuge" begins: *USA Today*, July 9, 1993, article titled "Abortion Clinics Nationwide Brace for Protests."

Heavy rains flooding coincide with Operation Rescue: *New York Times*, July 10, 1993, front page article titled "Flooded by Endless Rainfall, Midwest Braces for Still More."

Confirmation of Ginsburg as pro-abortion Justice: *USA Today*, July 22, 1993, article titled "Ginsburg Affirms Right to Abortion."

Five senators make pro-abortion statement: *USA Today*, July 22, 1993, article titled "5 Senate Women Vow Abortion Fight."

January 1994

Earthquake: *Los Angeles Times*, January 18, 1994, front page article titled "33 Die, Many Hurt in 6.6 Quake."

Location of earthquake a mystery: *USA Today*, January 31, 1994, article titled "Experts Try to Put a Face on No-Name Fault."

Earthquake had a "one-two punch": *USA Today*, January 26, 1994, article titled "Quake Packed a One-Two Punch."

Power of the earthquake: *USA Today*, January 31, 1994, article titled "Experts Try to Put a Face on No-Name Fault."

Destruction of pornography industry: Associated Press article, January 28, 1994, article titled "Quake Affects Porn Industry"; *The Wanderer*, St. Paul, MN, unknown date, article titled "L.A. Quake Rattles Porno Industry."

310,000 abortions—California: *USA Today*, June 20, 1992, article titled "Abortion Laws State by State."

March 1994

"Holy Week Passion for Life"—Birmingham, AL: *Birmingham Post-Herald Reporter*, March 25, 1994, article titled "Abortion Foes, Clinics Gird for Conflict."

Homosexual's activity at protest: Information obtained from interview of Operation Rescue's leader of event.

Tornadoes worst this century: *USA Today*, March 28, 1994, article titled "Day of Prayer Turns to Terror."

June 1994

Plunge of dollar starting June 17, 1994: *USA Today*, June 27, 1994, page 1B, article titled "Dollar Puts Summer Rally in Deep Freeze." (This article also covers the loss of the stock market during this week.)

Headline articles: "Dollar Plunges Worldwide, Threatening U.S. Recovery" —*The Sun*, Baltimore, MD, June 22, 1994, front page; "Dollar Puts Summer Rally in Deep Freeze"—*USA Today*, June 27, 1994; "Dollar's Slide Could Hamstring Economy"—*USA Today*, June 28, 1994.

Gay Olympic Games, New York City, June 18–25, 1994: *New York Times*, June 19, 1994, article titled "Ceremony Helps Start Gay Games-Week of Sports Events Opens at Wein Stadium."

AT&T sponsored the Gay Games: See above article

Homosexuals marched naked: New York City Police officers' eyewitness accounts.

July 1994

Operation Rescue—Little Rock, AR: *USA Today*, July 7, 1994, article titled "Protesters Target Clinton's Home State."

Floods in Georgia: *USA Today*, July 7, 1994, article titled "The Heavens Swamp the Earth."

Destruction of floods: *USA Today*, July 11, 1994, article titled "In Georgia, a Sea of Misery" and *New York Times*, July 9, 1994, article titled "Georgia Tries to Make Sense of Flood That Comes Once in 500 Years."

Atlanta and brutality against pro-life demonstrators: Consent order signed by Senior United States District Judge Marvin Shoob.

September 1994

Earthquake during Cairo conference: *USA Today*, September 13, 1994, article titled "Earthquake."

October 1994

Texas floods: *USA Today*, October 19, 1994, article titled "Texans Watch Luck Wash Away—Houston Area Struggles With Deadly Floods."

Judge Eileen O'Neill's injunction: *National Rescue Update*, September 1992, article titled "Houston Judge Declares Gospel Free Zone."

Protesters released on writ of habeas corpus: *National Rescue Update*, October 1992, article titled "Victory in Houston."

Civil Suits against Operation Rescue: *USA Today*, May 9, 1994, article titled "Abortion Foes Await $1 Million Decision."

Planned Parenthood aborts 120,000 babies nationwide: *National Right to Life News*, September 24, 1991, article titled "Planned Parenthood Image Sharply Contrast with Reality."

November 1994

Damage by Tropical Storm Gordon: *USA Today*, November 18, 1994, article titled "Gordon's Florida Onslaught," and November 21, 1994, article titled "Weakened Gordon Aims at Florida Again."

January 1995

Flooding in California: *USA Today*, January 11, 1995, article titled "Top to Bottom, Calif.'s Soaked."

Amount of damage and 500-year flood: National Public Radio (NPR), unknown date, January 1995, news stories about the floods in California.

April 1995

Murder rate in New Orleans: *USA Today*, April 12, 1995, article titled "There's Hope in New Orleans."

Operation Rescue prayer that there would be no murders during the week: Operation Rescue national newsletter, May 1, 1995.

Earthquake in West Texas: *Houston Post*, April 14, 1995, front page article titled "Earthquake Jolts N.M., West Texas."

August–October 1995

19 named storms during hurricane season: *USA Today*, November 30, 1995, article titled " '95 Storm Season Almost Blew Away All the Records."

$193 million approved for family planning: Associated Press article dated August 3, 1995, article titled "House Democrats, GOP Moderates Defeat Bid to Kill Family Planning Program."

Hurricane Erin slams into Florida: Associated Press article dated August 3, 1995, article titled "Hurricane Erin Rips Through Central Florida."

Supreme Court refuses to hear challenge to FACE law: *USA Today*, October 3, 1995, article titled "Supreme Court Refuses to Hear Suit Challenging Abortion Clinic Access Law."

Movement of Hurricane Opal chart of hurricane: NOAA, National Hurricane Center, October 6, 1995.

Destruction of the hurricane: *Harrisburg Patriot*, October 6, 1995, article titled "Opal Leaves 'Utter Destruction.'"; *USA Today*, October 6, 1995, article titled "Panhandle 'Like a War Zone.'"

January 1996

Newspaper reports flooding in PA: *Harrisburg Patriot-News*, January 21, 1996, front page article titled "River of Destruction"; *Harrisburg Patriot-News*, January 23, 1996, front page article titled "Flood's Effect Crushing."

Newspapers reporting Supreme Court decision: *Harrisburg Patriot-News*,

January 23, 1996, front page section B, article titled "State Loses Appeal on Abortion" and "Abortion Foes Mark Anniversary of Court's Roe vs. Wade Ruling."

March 1996

Stock market plunge of 171 points: *Washington Post*, March 9, 1996, front page article titled "Job Gains Send Market Plunging."

Jury acquits Kevorkian: *Washington Post*, March 9, 1996, front page article titled "Jury Acquits Kevorkian in Two Suicides."

Federal court overtures assisted suicide ban: *San Francisco Chronicle*, March 7, 1996, article titled "Court Voids Ban on Aid in Suicides."

May 1996

Quote about drought: *New York Times*, May 20, 1996, front page article titled "Worst Drought Since '30s Grips Plains," subtitled "Wheat Farmers and Ranchers Are Ruined."

Statements from Texas Agriculture Commissioner about destruction of drought: *USA Today*, May 23, 1996, page three article titled "Texas Drought May Be Crisis of the Century."

October 1995 was promoted as Gay/Lesbian History Month by the National Education Association (NEA): This was reported on various radio news reports during October 1995.

President Clinton promotes homosexual legislation: Associated Press article dated October 21, 1995, titled "Anti-Gay Job Bias Decried," subtitled "Clinton voices support of bill."

July 1996

Hurricane Bertha: *New York Times*, July 13, 1996, front page article titled "Anticipation Ends as Hurricane Slams Into North Carolina's Coast."

Hawaii on verge of legalizing same-sex marriages: *Harrisburg Patriot-News*, May 1, 1996, article titled "Same-Sex Marriage Near to Gaining Legal Status."

House vote on Defense of Marriage Act: *New York Times*, July 13, 1996, front page article titled "House Passes Bar to U.S. Sanction of Gay Marriage."

Stock market plunge: *New York Times*, July 12, 1996, front page business section, article titled "Stocks Plunge on Weaker Corporate Earnings and Rate Fears"; *New York Times*, July 16, 1996, front page article titled "Stocks Plunge as Dow Loses 161 and Technology Rout Continues."

September 1996

Hurricane Fran: *USA Today*, September 5, 1996, front page article titled "Hurricane Fran Expected Ashore Tonight."

Devastation: *The Patriot-News, Evening*, September 6, 1996, front page article titled "Fran Kills at Least 11."

Washington, D.C., flooding: *The Baltimore Sun*, September 10, 1996, article titled "D.C. Traffic Headaches Rise as Potomac Slowly Retreats."

Defense of Marriage Act: *USA Today*, September 5, 1996, article titled "Marriage Act Mired in Amendments"; *New York Times*, September 6, 1996, article titled "Anti-Discrimination Proposal Delays Senate Vote on Bill Opposing Same-Sex Marriage."

March 1997

Senate passes family planning: *New York Times*, February 26, 1997, article titled "Senate Backs Family-Planning Overseas."

Tornadoes: *USA Today*, March 3, 1997, front page article titled "Tornadoes, Flooding Kill 42"; *USA Today*, March 3, 1997, article titled "Storms' Death Toll Expected to Rise."

Record flooding: *Weatherwise Magazine*, June 1997, pages 7, 9; *Harrisburg Patriot-News*, March 6, 1997, article titled "Midwest Flooding Showing

No Ebb."

July 1997

Operation Rescue: *Dayton Daily News*, July 19, 1997, article titled "Group Ends Week of Protests."

Hurricane Danny: *New York Times*, July 21, 1997, article titled "Day of Wind and Rain That Lasts Too Long"; Associated Press, July 21, 1997, article titled "In Deep Water."

October 1997

Partial-birth abortion ban: *The Harrisburg Patriot-News*, October 8, 1997, article titled "Congress OKs Partial-Birth Abortion Ban."

Stock market crash: *New York Times*, October 28, 1997, article titled "Stocks Fall 554 Points Off 7%."

December 1997

New abortion technique: Lead story reported on television evening news; *Harrisburg Patriot-News*, December 21, 1997, front page article titled "New Early Abortion Technique on the Rise."

Storm in Texas: Second story reported on television evening news; Associated Press, December 21, 1997, article titled "Eight People Die in Floods."

January 1998

Clinton reverses abortion restrictions: *New York Times*, January 22, 1993, article titled "Clinton Orders Reversal of Abortion Restrictions Left by Reagan and Bush."

Clinton sex scandal revealed: *Harrisburg Patriot-News*, January 22, 1998, front page article titled "Outraged Clinton Denies New Charges."

March 1998

Supreme Court rejected abortion case: *New York Times*, March 24, 1998, front page article titled "Supreme Court Turns Down Late-Term Abortion Case."

Shootings: *The Harrisburg Patriot-News*, March 25, 1998, front page article titled "School Ambush in Arkansas."

Euthanasia death: *USA Today*, March 26, 1998, article titled "First Known Suicide Under Ore. Law Revealed"

June 1998

Gay Days 1998 at Disneyland: information from Gay98Day website on Internet (*www.gayday.com*)

President Clinton's letter of congratulations regarding Gay and Lesbian Pride Celebration, 1998: Gay98Day website (*www.gayday.com/clinton_message.asp*)

Review of Gay Day schedule: information from Gay98Day website on Internet (*www.gayday. com/schedule.asp*)

Operation Rescue protest at Barnes and Noble bookstore, Disneyland, and city of Orlando: Associated Press, June 2, 1998, article titled "Abortion Opponents Protest Clinic"

Operation Rescue prayer vigil ends on June 6, 1998 at 2:30 p.m.: Telephone conversation with Rusty Thomas who coordinated the event at Disneyland.

Fires start at 2:30 p.m. on June 6, 1998: *Orlando Sentinel*, June 7, 1998, article titled "Hot, Dry Weather Sparks Blazes"

Extent of the fires: *Harrisburg Patriot News*, July 7, 1998, front page article titled "Florida Fires"

Fires cause $1 billion in crop damages: *Orlando Sentinel*, July 8, 1998, article titled "This Year's Disasters Could Cost $1 billion"

Gov. Chiles declares state of emergency on June 7, 1998: Associated Press, June 7, 1998, article titled "Florida Gripped by Wild Fires"

Florida declared a disaster area by president on June 19: Federal Emergency

Management Agency (FEMA), June 19, 1997, article titled "President Orders Federal Aid for Florida Fires"

40,000 residents allowed to return home: *Harrisburg Patriot News*, July 7, 1998, front page article titled "40,000 Get OK To Go Home"

The halting of the ban against partial-birth abortions: Associated Press, June 30, 1998, article titled "New Abortion Law Won't be Enforced"

July 1998

Stock market reaches all time high of 9337: *USA Today*, July 24, 1998, article titled "Market Stress Mounts Over Asia, Earnings"

On July 23, 1998 stock market drops 195 points (sixth-biggest drop): Reuters News Service, July 23, 1998, article titled "Stocks Take the Fourth Hit in a Row"

House votes on partial-birth abortion on July 23, 1998: *USA Today*, July 24, 1998, front page article titled "House Votes to Override Veto of Late-term Abortion Ban"

Market plunges 513 points on August 31, 1998 for 1800 point loss: Associated Press, August 31, 1998, article titled "Dow Off 513, Nasdaq Down 140"

Radio reports on July 23, 1998: Unknown radio station reporting the news for the day

Three stories together in *USA Today*: *USA Today*, July 24, 1998, front page heading "Newsline" (the stories are Wall Street—Heat's Toll—Abortion)

August 1998

San Francisco passed domestic partners ordinance: *USA Today*, August 11, 1998, article under heading Nationline titled "Gay Rights"

San Francisco earthquake: *USA Today*, August 13, 1998, article under the heading Nationline titled "5.4 Magnitude Earthquake Rocks San Francisco Area"

Warning of greater earthquake to come: *New York Times*, August 13, 1998, article titled "Gentle Quake Rattles Nerves and Buildings in Bay Area"

January 1999

Powerful tornadoes hit Arkansas and Tennessee do $1 billion in damage: *Washington Post*, January 23, 1999, article titled "Tornadoes Rip Through Arkansas, Tennessee; 8 People Killed"

Storm set records: *Washington Post*, January 23, 1999, article titled "Tornadoes Rip Through Arkansas, Tennessee; 8 People Killed" and Associated Press, February 9, 1999, article titled "January Sets Tornado Record"

Chelsea's tree house destroyed: Associated Press, January 23, 1999, article titled "Twisters Rip South, Wreck Chelsea's Old Tree House"

Speech by ex-Senator Dale Bumpers: from government website which supplied the complete transcript of the speech

292 warnings: *Arkansas Democrat Gazette*, January 23, 1999, article titled "7 Die as 38 Tornadoes Rip 750 Homes, Leave 63,500 Without Power."

Training of tornadoes: *Washington Post*, January 23, 1999, article titled "Tornadoes Rip Through Arkansas, Tennessee; 8 People Killed"

Hillary Clinton speech before NARAL: Associated Press, January 22, 1999, article titled "Clinton Seeks Abortion Clinic Funds"

Arkansas declared a disaster area: Associated Press, January 23, 1999, article titled "Tenn., Ark. Declared Disaster Area."

March 1999

Homosexual activism: *Washington Post*, March 22, 1999, article titled "Calling for Equality to Begin at Home"

WorldNetDaily.com, undated, article titled "Homosexual activism on overdrive 300 activities in 50 states next week"

Maryland legislation: *Washington Post*, March 24, 1999, article titled "Md.

House Likely to Pass Gay Rights Legislation"

Air attack of Serbia: *Washington Post*, March 25, 1999, article titled "U.S. Allies Launch Air Attack On Yugoslav Military Targets."

Attack on Serbia changes political landscape: *Boston Globe*, April 8, 1999, article titled "Russian Military Sees A Balkan Opportunity." August 25, 1999, article titled "Moscow and China cement anti-Nato pact." *NewsMax.com*, January 14, 2000, article titled "Russia raises nuclear threat."

April 1999

Operation Rescue: *New York Times*, April 20, 1999, article titled, "Protests in Buffalo Continue, with Police and Media Outnumbering abortion Opponents."

Shootings in high schools: *New York Times*, April 21, 1999, article titled "2 Youths in Colorado School Said to Gun Down As Many As 23"

July 1999

Drought of 1999: *Sunday Patriot-News*, July 25, 1999, front page article titled "Anatomy of a Drought"; *Washington Post*, July 30, 1999, article titled "Md. Under Drought Emergency"; *USA Today*, June 25, 1999, article titled "Record-dry weather leaves farms parched"; Associated Press, August 8, 1999, article titled "A Look at Drought Conditions"

Homosexual legislation: *USA Today*, June 25, 1999, article titled "Gay Rights"

June designated as Gay Pride Month: On June 2, 2000, President Clinton made June officially Gay and Lesbian Pride Month by a proclamation. It had been unofficial until then. Letter from the president dated June 2, 2000.

August 1999

Boy Scouts: *USA Today*, August 5, 1999, front page article titled "Court rejects ouster of gay Scout leader"

Drought: Associated Press, August 5, 1999, article titled "Drought Plagues Mid-Atlantic"

October 1999

Homosexual legislation in California: *Los Angeles Times*, October 3, 1999, article titled "Davis Signs 3 Bills Supporting Domestic Partners, Gay Rights"

California to lead nation in homosexual rights: Associated Press, October 14, 1999, article titled "Calif. Covets Trailblazer Image"

Earthquake: *Los Angeles Times*, October 17, 1999, front page article titled "7.0 Earthquake in Mojave Desert Rocks Southland"; Associated Press, October 19, 1999, article titled "Quake Fault Lines Said Conversation"

March 2000

Texas prayer case: *USA Today*, dated March 29, 2000, article titled "Pre-game prayers go to high court"

Tornado: *USA Today*, article March 29, 2000, article titled, "Tornado rips through downtown Fort Worth"

April 2000

Partial-birth abortion: *Washington Post*, April 5, 2000, editorial article titled "Partial-Birth Posturing"

Stock market upheaval: *Washington Post*, April 5, 2000, front page article titled "A Wild Ride on Wall Street"; *USA Today*, April 5, 2000, article titled "Markets' wildest ride" and "Bear market rumbles on Wall Street"

February 2001

Violence at Mardi Gras: *Seattle Post-Intelligencer*, article titled "Special Report: Violence at the Mardi Gras," *http://seattlep-i.nwsource.com/specials/mardigras/*

Earthquake: EQE International report titled "Seattle, Wash Earthquake of 2/

28/2001 M6.8," website, *www.eqe.com.*

Earthquake and Mardi Gras together: *USA Today*, March 1, 2001, page 3, articles titled "Seattle glad wallop wasn't worse" and "Mardi Gras injuries, arrests."

Seismologists and Sin

Joshua Tree Quake: Article titled "Joshua Tree Earthquake, Southern Calif. Earthquake Center," *www.scecdc.org/joshuatr.html*

Landers Quake: Article titled "Landers Earthquake, Southern Calif. Earthquake Center," *www.scecdc.org/landersq.html.* Article titled "The Landers and Big Bear Earthquakes" EQE International, *www.eqe.com/publications/bigbear/bigbear.htm.*

Hector Mine Quake: Article titled "Special Report: Hector Mine Earthquake," October 16, 1999, United States Geological Survey, *www.pasadena.wr.usgs.gov/hector/report.html;* Article titled "Preliminary Report on the 10/16/1999 M7.1 Hector Mine, California Earthquake," scientists from the U.S. Geological Survey, Southern Calif. Center, *www.pasadena.wr.gov/hector/hector_srl.html;* Article titled "The M7.1 Hector Mine Earthquake," October 16, 1999, Radarcast website, *www.radarcast.homestead.com;* Article titled "Scientists: Quake faults lines are talking to each other," October 19, 1999, The Associated Press; Article titled "Post-Quake stress may cause quakes," May 9, 2001, Associated Press; Article titled "Earthquake: Shock delay," by Elizabeth H. Hearn, May 10, 2001, *Nature Journal,* vol. 411, page 150, and article titled "Delayed triggering of the 1999 Hector Mine earthquake by viscoelastic stress transfer," by Andrew M. Freed, page 180.

San Andreas Fault: Article titled "The San Andreas Fault," United States Geological Survey, *http://pubs.usgs.gov/gip/earthq3/safaultgip.html*

Background of Dr. Tiller: *Kansas for Life Newsletter,* May 1991, article titled "Exposé on Abortion."

Activity at Dr. Tiller's Abortion Center: *New York Times,* August 26, 1991, article titled "25,000 Opponents of Abortion Rally in Wichita.

Hurricane Bob, abortion, and homosexuality: *USA Today*, August 20, 1991, p. 6A, articles titled "Bob batters Eastern Seaboard," "Court challenges military ban on gays," and "Abortion foes flock to Heartland rally."

Chapter Two

November 1991

Opening of Madrid peace talks: *USA Today*, October 31, 1991, front page article titled "Delegates Bring Optimism to Table."

The land of Israel key issue: *USA Today*, November 1, 1997, front page article titled "One-on-One Peace Talks Next."

Storm developments and results: *New York Times*, November 1, 1997, article titled "Nameless Storm Swamps the Shoreline"; *USA Today*, November 1, 1997, front page article titled "East Coast Hit Hard by Rare Storm" and article titled "Bob the Sequel a Smash (Maine to Florida under siege)."

President Bush's home smashed by the storm: *New York Times*, November 1, 1997, article titled "Stormy Waves Heavily Damage Bush Vacation Compound in Southern Maine."

The book, *The Perfect Storm*, by Sebastian Junger, 1997, HarperCollins Publisher. The power of the storm pages 118, 119.

Rare condition create the Perfect Storm: Associated Press, June 29, 2000, article titled "Perfect Storm Recalled."

August 1992

Hurricane Andrew and Madrid peace plan together: *USA Today*, August 24, 1992, front page articles titled "1 Million Flee Andrew; Monster Storm Targets Fla.," and "Mideast Peace Talks to Resume on Positive Note."

Damage done by Andrew: *USA Today*, September 14, 1992, article titled "Tale of the Hurricanes"; *USA Today*, September 18, 1992, article titled "Andrew 3rd-Worst Storm."

September 1993

Hurricane Emily and dividing the land of Israel: *New York Times*, September 1, 1993, front page articles (these articles touched each other) titled "Israel and PLO Ready To Declare Joint Recognition," and "Hurricane Hits the Outer Banks, As Thousands Seek Safety Inland."

January 1994

President Clinton and Assad meet in Geneva: *Harrisburg Patriot-News*, January 17, 1994, front page article titled "Clinton: Syria Set for Peace."

Earthquake in L.A.: *Los Angeles Times*, January 18, 1994, front page article titled "33 Die, Many Hurt in 6.6 Quake." (For more details of this earthquake, see chapter one, January 1994 heading.)

March 1997

Arafat arrives in America and meets with Clinton: *New York Times*, March 3, 1997, article titled "Welcoming Arafat, Clinton Rebukes Israel."

Arafat on speaking tour: *New York Times*, March 6, 1997, article titled "Arafat Lobbies U.S. Against Israel's Housing Plan."

For information about tornadoes and floods, see chapter one, March 1997 heading.

Security Counsel's resolution of March 6, 1997: *New York Times*, March 7, 1997, article titled "U.S. Vetoes U.N. Criticism of Israel's Construction Plan."

General Assembly resolution of March 13, 1997: *New York Times*, March 14, 1997, article titled "Israel's Plan of Jerusalem Is Condemned by Assembly."

Security Counsel's resolution of March 21, 1997: *New York Times*, March 22, 1997, "U.S. Again Vetoes a Move by U.N. Condemning Israel."

General Assembly resolution of April 25, 1997: *New York Times*, April 25, 1997, article titled "Israel Warned to Halt Housing for Jews."

General Assembly resolution of July 15, 1997: *New York Times*, July 16, 1997, article titled "U.N. Renews Censure of New Israeli Housing in East Jerusalem."

Stock market reaches all-time high: *USA Today*, March 12, 1997, article titled "Dow Achieves Record Despite Rate Fears."

Stock market falls 160 Points: *USA Today*, March 14, 1997, article titled "Dow Plunges 160 Points on Rate Fears."

Stock market stabilizes and begins rebound: *USA Today*, April 15, 1997, article titled "Stock Market Summary."

Prime Minister Netanyahu meets with Clinton: *New York Times*, April 8, 1997, article titled "Netanyahu Holds White House Talks."

July 1997

Devaluation of Thailand's currency: *New York Times*, July 2, 1997, article titled "Thais Effectively Devalue Their Wobbly Currency."

U.N. resolution, July 15, 1997: *NY Times*, July 16, 1997, article titled "UN Renews Censure of New Israeli Housing in East Jerusalem."

Stock market crash: *New York Times*, October 27, 1997, article titled "Stocks Fall 554 Points, Off 7% Forcing Suspension in Trading."

Asian crisis affects world economy: *USA Today*, October 24, 1997, article titled

"Market Dive Circles Globe."

January 1998

Clinton meets with Netanyahu: *New York Times*, January 22, 1998, article titled "U.S. and Israel Talk Mainly of More Talks"; *USA Today*, January 22, 1998, article titled "A Mideast Battle for Good Press."

Clinton meets with Arafat: *USA Today*, January 23, 1998, article titled "Arafat Calls Talks Encouraging."

Clinton's sex scandal breaks during meeting with Netanyahu: *New York Times*, January 22, 1998. Front page article titled "Subpoenas Sent as Clinton Denies Reports of an Affair with Aide at White House."

Clinton coldly treats Netanyahu and Netanyahu returns as a hero: *New York Times*, January 30, 1998, article titled "Analysis: In Clinton Crisis, Netanyahu Gains, Arafat Loses."

House votes to begin impeachment of president: Associated Press, October 8, 1998, article titled, "House Approves Impeachment Inquiry"

September 1998

Clinton to met with Netanyahu and Arafat: *New York Times*, September 25, 1998, article titled "Clinton to See Netanyahu and Arafat Next Week"

Hurricane gains strength: *USA Today*, September 25, 1998, front page article titled "Georges Gaining Strength: Killer Storm Zeros in on Key West"

Secretary of State Albright meets with Arafat in NYC: *New York Times*, September 28, 1998, article titled "US Is Hoping to Announce Details on Israel-Palestine Talks"

Hurricane Georges slams into Gulf Coast: *New York Times*, September 28, 1998, front page article titled "Recharged Hurricane Batters Gulf Coast With 110 m.p.h. Winds"

Hurricane Lingers on Gulf Coast: *USA Today*, September 29, 1998, front page article titled "Georges Lingers"

President Clinton meets with Arafat and Netanyahu in White House: *USA Today*, September 29, 1998, front page article titled "Meeting Puts Mideast Talks Back in Motion"

Hurricane and Mideast peace talks together: *New York Times*, September 29, 1998, front pages articles titled "U.S., Israel and Arafat Inch Toward Pact" and "Floods Trap Hundreds"

Arafat speaks at United Nations: *New York Times*, September 29, 1998, article titled "Arafat, at U.N., Urges Backing for Statehood"

Hurricane causes $1 billion in damage: *USA Today*, September 30, 1998, article titled "Hurricane Racks Up $1 Billion in Damage"

October 1998

Netanyahu and Arafat met in United States: *Harrisburg Patriot News*, October 15, 1998, front page article titled "Time Is Running Out in Mideast"

Israel to give away 13 percent of the land: *New York Times*, October 24, 1998, front page article titled "Arafat and Netanyahu in Pact on Next Steps Toward Peace; Modest Deal to Rebuild Trust"

Powerful storms hit Texas: *Harrisburg Patriot News*, October 18, 1998, article titled "4 Killed as Storms, Floods, Tornado Ravage Parts of Texas"

Extent of the flooding and damage: *New York Times*, October 20, 1998, article titled "Record Flooding Kills at Least 14 in Central Texas," and *USA Today*, October 22, 1998, article titled "Hope Dwindles in Flooded Texas"

Texas declared a disaster area by president: News release, October 21, 1998 from FEMA. Release was titled "President Declares Major Disaster for Texas: Twenty Counties Designated for Aid to Flood Victims"

This disaster and Mideast talks together on front page of newspaper: *New York Times*, October 20, 1998, articles titled "Clinton Keeps Up Hope of

Mideast Talks" and "Knee-deep in the San Jacinto"

November 1998

Stock Market reached all time high on November 23, 1998: Associated Press News Service, December 10, 1998, article titled "Stocks Fall for Third Straight Session"

Clinton and Arafat met on November 30 to raise money for Palestinians: *Baltimore Sun*, December 1, 1998, front page article titled "Nations Pledge $3 Billion in Aid to Palestinians"

Stock market drops 216 points on November 30: *Baltimore Sun*, De-cember 1, 1998, front page article titled "Expected Correction Cools Off Wall St." (The articles about Arafat and the stock market were next to each other on the front page)

European stock markets crash: Associated Press News Service, December 2, 1998, article titled "UK Stocks Hammered"

December 1998

Judicial Committee votes on December 11 for three articles of impeach-ment: *USA Today*, December 11, 1998, front page article titled "Panel Sets Stage for Historic Vote on Impeachment"

Clinton on route to Israel while the fourth article of impeachment is being voted: Associated Press News Service, December 12, 1998, article titled "Clinton Heads for Israel," and article titled "Fourth Impeach-ment Article Debated"

Clinton is the first president to visit Palestinian-controlled area: *USA Today*, December 12, 1998, front page article titled "Clinton Fights for Mideast Agreement"

Clinton's visit gives status to a Palestinian state: *USA Today*, December 12, 1998, front page article titled "Peace Hits Snag Despite Vote"

On December 19 Clinton impeached by the House of Representatives: *Harrisburg Patriot-News*, December 20, 1998, titled "Impeached"

March 1999

On March 23, Arafat meets with President Clinton: *New York Times*, March 24, 1999, article titled "Arafat Says Little on Clinton Meeting."

On March 23, stock market falls 219 points: *Washington Post*, March 24, 1999, article titled "Dow Takes Biggest Fall in 2 Months."

Air attack of Serbia: *Washington Post*, March 25, 1999, article titled "U.S. Allies Launch Air Attack on Yugoslav Military Targets."

Attack on Serbia changes political landscape: *Boston Globe*, April 8, 1999, article titled "Russian Military Sees a Balkan Opportunity"; August 25, 1999, article titled "Moscow and China cement anti-Nato pact"; *NewsMax.com*, dated January 14, 2000, article titled "Russia raises nuclear threat."

May 1999

Clinton and the Palestinian State: Associated Press, May 4, 1999, article titled "Clinton Encourages Arafat."

Power and wind speed of the tornadoes: *USA Today*, May 11, 1999, article titled "318-mph storm wind fastest ever"; *USA Today*, may 5, 1999, article titled "Disasters declared in two states"; *Harrisburg Patriot-News*, May 5, 1999, article titled "20 hours of terror."

September 1999

Hurricane Dennis: *Harrisburg Patriot-News*, September 4, 1999, front page article titled "Enough already N.C. tires of Dennis."

Middle East meetings regarding Israel: *Harrisburg Patriot-News*, September 4, 1999, front page article titled "Talks yield reworking of Wye pact."

Hurricane Floyd: *Harrisburg Patriot-News*, September 19, 1999, article titled

"Floodwaters devastating N.Carolina."

Floyd Strengthens: Associated Press, September 13, 1999, article titled "Floyd Strengthens, Near Bahamas."

Middle East talks open: Associated Press, September 13, 1999, article titled "Israel, Palestinians To Open Talks."

Arafat meets with Clinton: Associated Press, September 22, 1999, article titled "Clinton Hosts Arafat at White House."

Stock market crash sets record: Reuters, September 23, 1999, article titled "Dow, Nasdaq Take Late-Day Tumble"

October 1999

Eviction of Israeli settlers: *New York Times*, October 16, 1999, front page article titled "On the West Bank, a Mellow View of Eviction."

Stock market crash: *New York Times*, October 16, 1999, front page article titled "Big Selloff Caps Dow's Worst Week Since October '89."

Earthquake: *Los Angeles Times*, October 17, 1999, front page article titled "7.0 Earthquake in Mojave Desert Rocks Southland."

Hurricane Irene: *USA Today*, October 18, 1999, article titled "Battered North Carolina suffers third hurricane in two months."

January 2000

Meetings: *New York Times*, January 4, 2000, front page article titled "Israel and Syria Return to Search for a Major Accord."

Stock market crash: *USA Today*, January 5, 2000, front page article titled "Market sell-off was overdue."

Turbulent stock week: *New York Times*, January 8, 2000, article titled "The 3 Main U.S. Stock Gauges Rally to End a Turbulent Week."

April 2000

Barak meets with Clinton: Associated Press, April 12, 2000, article titled "Israel OKs US Involvement in Talks."

Stock market collapse: *New York Times*, April 15, 2000, front page article titled "Stock Market in Step Drop as Worried Investors Flee; NASDAQ Has Its Worst Week"

June 2000

Arafat meets with Clinton: Associated Press, June 15, 2000, article titled "Clinton Welcomes Arafat for Talks."

Stock market fall: Reuters, June 16, 2000, article titled "Banks Lead Blue Chips Plunge."

July–August 2000

Camp David meetings: Reuters, November 21, 2000, article titled "Jerusalem Sovereignty Debated in Public Amid Talks"; Associated Press, dated July 20, 2000, article titled "Jerusalem at Heart of Mideast Talks."

Forest fires: Associated Press, August 3, 2000, article titled "Fire Season Storms Into West"; Reuters, August 27, 2000, article titled "U.S. Wildfires Converge in 'Perfect Storm.'"

Drought: Associated Press, July 28, 2000, article titled "Bush Declares Texas Disaster Areas."

September–December 2000

Fighting erupts at Temple Mount: *New York Times*, September 30, 2000, front page, article titled "Battle at Jerusalem Holy Site Leaves 4 Dead and 200 Hurt.'"

Collapse of Barak's government: *Washington Post*, December 10, 2000, front page, article titled "Israeli Prime Minister Says He Will Resign."

Presidential election: *New York Times*, November 10, 2000, front page, article titled "Gore Campaign Vows Court Fight Over Vote with Florida's Outcome Still Up in the Air."

Arafat meets with Clinton: *New York Times*, November 10, 2000, article titled "Arafat-Clinton Talks in Washington Yield No Progress."

Elections set in Israel: *New York Times*, December 11, 2000, front page, article titled "Opening Campaign Netanyahu Invokes Will of the Nation."

Election resolved: *New York Times*, December 11, 2000, front page, article titled "Bush-Gore Is Now in the Hands of the Supreme Court."

Chapter Three

All the charts in this chapter were from the book *America: To Pray Or Not To Pray*" by David Barton. Charts used by permission. This book is highly recommended. The book can be ordered from Wall Builder Press, P.O. Box 397, Aledo, TX 76008, (817)441-6044.

Chapter Four

Chart: *The Index of Social Health: Information Obtained from Monitoring the Social Well-Being of the Nation*, 1994, Fordham Institute for Innovation in Social Policy, Fordham University Graduate Center, Tarrytown, New York, 10591.

36.6 million victims of crimes: *USA Today*, November 23, 1993, articled titled "Criminals Have Hurt 37 Million Since '73."

U.S. prison population reaches one million: *New York Times*, October 28, 1994, article titled "Ranks of Inmates Reach One Million in a 2-Decade Rise."

Crime rate in U.S. and Washington, D.C.: *New York Times*, October 28, 1994, chart titled "State By State, Behind Bars." This rate was for period ending June 30, 1994.

Abortion rate in U.S. and Washington, D.C.: *Family Planning Perspectives*, volume 26, number 3, May/June 1994, article titled "Abortion Services in the United States, 1991 and 1992."

Child abuse rates in the U.S.: *USA Today*, January 24, 1992, article titled "Infant Murders Climbing," and attached chart titled "Child Abuse: Growing Problem in the USA."

Chart—Real GNP: The Bank Credit Analyst.

Chart—Constant 1992 Wages: *The Capitalist Manifesto*, James Dale Davidson, page 8, Strategic Investment, 824 East Baltimore Street, Baltimore ,MD 21201.

Increase in federal deficit: *USA Today*, February 12, 1993, article titled "Federal Deficit Has a Life of Its Own."

Poverty rate in U.S. for 1993: *The Patriot-News*, Harrisburg, PA, October 7, 1994, article titled "U.S. Poverty Rate Tops 39 Million, Highest Number Since Early 1960s."

Statistics about bear stock markets taken from newspaper article titled "Growling on Wall Street," *USA Today*, page 1B, April 4, 1994.

The Homosexual Connection: New York Times, December 16, 1973, article titled "Psychiatrists, in a Shift, Declare Homosexuality No Mental Illness"

Chapter Five
Abortion and Breast Cancer: The Deadly Link

Rutgers University's pro-homosexual position: *The Harrisburg Patriot-News*, January 16, 1994, article titled "Colleges on Cutting Edge of Gay Acceptance."

Washington State allows homosexuals to adopt children: *USA Today*, September 21, 1993, article titled "Judge Opens Door for Gay Couple to Adopt."

San Francisco and Massachusetts recognize homosexual relationships: *USA*

Today, September 24, 1992, article titled "Mass. Gives Benefits to Unmarried Couples."

30 studies have established the abortion/breast cancer link. For an exhaustive study, contact Life Dynamics, Inc., PO Box 185, Lewisville, TX 75067. 214/436-3885.

182,00 women per year develop breast cancer and 45,000 die: *The Patriot-News*, April 17, 1994, article titled "Halting Confusion Over Breast Cancer."

Women have 10% risk of developing breast cancer: *National Right to Life News*, Suite 500, 1419 7th Street NW, Washington, D.C., March 30, 1994, article by Joel Brind, Ph.D., titled "Abortion and Breast Cancer."

Main media and pro-abortion supporters ignoring link between abortion and breast cancer: *National Right to Life News*, January 1995, article by Joel Brind, Ph.D. titled "Denial Digs in Deeper as Evidence Mounts of Increased Incidence of Breast Cancer in Women Who've Aborted."

Joel Brind Ph.D. unable to get his research published in USA. He was dismissed from positions after publishing article in foreign journal. Information from article titled "The Most Dangerous Secret in Medicine" by Susan Reith Swan, *Celebrate Life Magazine*, May/June 1996, American Life League, P.O. Box 1350, Stafford, VA 22555. 540/659-4171.

National Cancer Institute research: "Risk of Breast Cancer Among Young Women: Relationship to Induced Abortion," *Journal of the National Cancer Institute*, vol. 86, no. 21, November 2, 1994. Research quoted in the *National Right to Life News*, November 18, 1994, page 18, article titled "Mass Media Finally Reveal the Tip of the Iceberg," by Joel Brind, Ph.D.

Howard University study of black women who developed breast cancer: *National Right to Life News*, November 18, 1994, article titled "Mass Media Finally Reveal the Tip of the Iceberg."

50,000 cases of breast cancer linked to abortion: Article titled "Abortion and Breast Cancer," *National Right to Life News*, March 15, 1996.

French study of the risk of breast cancer due to multiple abortions: *National Right to Life News*, January 1995, article by Joel Brind, Ph.D., titled "Denial Digs in Deeper as Evidence Mounts of Increased Incidence of Breast Cancer in Women Who've Aborted."

Lithuania abortion–breast cancer study: "Breast Cancer in Lithuania," *The Lancet*, vol. 344, October 1, 1994, page 947. This article was quoted in the November 11, 1994, issue of *Communiqué*, P.O. Box 1350, Stafford, VA 22555, 703/659-4171.

Giving birth reduces breast cancer risk: *National Right to Life News*, December 7, 1993, page 5, article by Joel Brind, Ph.D. titled "Abortion and Breast Cancer."

Theory behind abortion–breast cancer risk: *National Right to Life News*, December 7, 1993, article titled "Abortion and Breast Cancer."

God Gave Them Over to a Reprobate Mind

AMA 1994 policy statement on homosexuality: *The New York Times*, December 25, 1994, article titled "AMA Adopts New Policy on Sexuality."

AT&T sponsored "Gay Olympic Games": *The New York Times*, June 19, 1994, article titled "Ceremony Helps Start Gay Games."

Median age of death rates for various groups and statistics for chart: Article titled "Medical Consequences of What Homosexuals Do," by Dr. Paul Cameron of the Family Research Institute (FRI), PO Box 2091, Washington, D.C. 20013. 703/690-8536. This article and all the articles from FRI have been reproduced and are available if you contact FRI.

Violence associated with homosexuality: Article titled "Violence and Homosexuality," by Dr. Paul Cameron.

Homosexual death rate studied back to 1858: "Medical Consequences of What Homosexuals Do."

Homosexual serial killers: *The Pink Swastika*, by Scott Lively and Kevin Abrams, Founders Publishing Corporation, 1995, page 174–176. This book is must reading. For a copy contact Book Offer, Box 5271, Salem, OR 97304. 800/828-2290.

Venereal disease rate among homosexuals: "Medical Consequences of What Homosexuals Do."

The End Thereof Are the Ways of Death

10,000 women die a year due to abortion related breast cancer: "The Deadly After-Effect of Abortion—Breast Cancer" by Dr. J. C. Willke.

Women in San Francisco have highest breast cancer rate in world: Associated Press article, December 7, 1994. This article was quoted in the December 23, 1994 issue of *Communiqué*.

The Reprobate Mind

Seminar sponsored by National Abortion Federation (NAF) on September 13–14, 1992, and information about Dr. Martin Haskell and D&X abortion technique: Letter dated June 30, 1993, from Douglas Johnson, Legislative Director, National Right to Life Committee, Inc.(NRLC), Suite 500, 419 7th Street, NW, Washington, DC 20004. The subject of the letter was new documentation on "D&X" abortions. Attached to this letter was a copy of Dr. Haskell's paper which he presented at this seminar. Illustration of the D&X (partial-birth) abortion is an artist's conception as displayed on the floor of the House of Representatives. This occurred during the debate of the partial-birth abortion ban.

80% of partial-birth abortions elective: Article titled "Abortion Method Set for Ban Is Used Rarely by Doctors," by Tamar Lewin, November 2, 1995, *New York Times*.

Letter from Brenda Shafer, R.N. dated July 9, 1995, to Congressman Tony Hall.

13,000 late term abortions performed annually: Article titled "Method to End 20-Week Pregnancy Stirs a Corner of the Abortion Debate," by Tamar Lewin, July 5, 1995, *New York Times*.

300–500 babies aborted yearly by D&X technique: Letter dated June 18, 1993, from Barbara Radford, executive director, National Abortion Federation, 1436 U Street NW, Suite 103, Washington, D.C. 20009.